At Sylvan, we believe that reading, writing, and vocabulary skills are more than language arts—they are the cornerstone of lifelong communication skills. We're glad you've chosen our resources to help your child build this crucial knowledge. Effective reading, writing, and vocabulary skills prepare your child for school, for a career, and for life.

At Sylvan, language arts instruction uses a step-by-step process with research-based and thought-provoking lessons. With success, students become more confident. With increasing confidence, students build even more success. That's why our Sylvan workbooks aren't like the others; we're laying out the roadmap for learning.

Included with your purchase is a coupon for a discount on our in-center service. As your child continues his academic journey, your local Sylvan Learning Center can partner with your family to ensure that your child remains a confident, successful, and independent learner.

The Sylvan Team

5th-Grade Super Reading Success

Published in the United States by Random House, Inc.,New York, and in Canada by Random House of Canada Limited, Toronto.

www.tutoring.sylvanlearning.com

Created by Smarterville Productions LLC
Cover and Interior Photos: Jonathan Pozniak
Cover and Interior Illustrations: Delfin Barral

First Edition

ISBN: 978-0-375-43019-0

Library of Congress Cataloging-in-Publication Data available upon request.

This book is available at special discounts for bulk purchases for sales promotions or premiums. For more information, write to Special Markets/Premium Sales, 1745 Broadway, MD 6-2, New York, New York 10019 or e-mail specialmarkets@randomhouse.com.

PRINTED IN CHINA

10 9 8 7 6 5 4 3 2 1

Vocabulary Contents

Reading Comprehension Contents

Writing Contents

Checking your answers is part of the learning.

Each section of the workbook begins with an easy-to-use Check It! strip.

1. Before beginning the activities, cut out the Check It! strip.
2. As you complete the activities on each page, check your answers.
3. If you find an error, you can correct it yourself.

Synonyms & Antonyms

1

Keywords

a•bun•dant–uh-BUHN-duhnt *adjective* present in large amou
or numbers
Synonyms: plentiful, full, ample. Antonyms: empty, lacking.

be•stow–bih-STOH *verb* to give or present something to someo
Synonyms: give, grant, award. Antonyms: take, get.

ea•ger–EE-ger *adjective* enthusiastic and impatiently excited
Synonyms: keen, anxious, impatient. Antonyms: indifferent, reluctant.

fra•grant–FRAY-gruhnt *adjective* having a pleasant smell
Synonyms: perfumed, scented, sweet smelling. Antonyms: musty, stinky

he•ro•ic–hih-ROH-ihk *adjective* 1. showing great bravery, daring, or courage 2. relating to a hero 3. large in size, power, or effect
Synonyms: brave, daring, mighty. Antonyms: cowardly, timid.

in•vade–ihn-VAYD *verb* 1. to enter by force with an army 2. to enter in great numbers or spread over
Synonyms: enter, attack, raid. Antonym: withdraw.

per•sist–per-SIHST *verb* 1. to continue steadily in spite of problems or difficulties 2. to continue to exist
Synonyms: continue, endure, last. Antonyms: discontinue, stop.

spec•ta•cle–SPEHK-tuh-kuhl *noun* a strange or interesting sight
Synonyms: scene, show, wonder. Antonyms: normality, ordinariness.

tri•umph–TRI-uhmf *noun* 1. a great win or achievement 2. a feeling of happiness and pride that comes from success
Synonyms: victory, win, success. Antonyms: loss, defeat.

vig•or•ous–VIHG-er-uhs *adjective* 1. very strong or active, physically or mentally 2. using or displaying great energy or force
Synonyms: active, forceful, energetic. Antonyms: weak, powerless.

Check It!

Page 2

Read & Replace

1. spectacle
2. heroic
3. eager
4. invade
5. fragrant
6. abundant
7. vigorous
8. persist
9. bestow
10. triumph

Page 3

Blank Out!

1. abundant
2. vigorous
3. eager
4. spectacle
5. bestow
6. fragrant
7. persist
8. invade
9. triumph
10. heroic

Page 4

Tic-Tac-Toe

1. stinky, dank, smelly
2. attack, seize, storm
3. extravaganza, marvel, wonder
4. last, continue, remain

Page 5

Criss Cross

ACROSS
2. fragrant
4. spectacle
7. heroic
8. bestow
9. triumph

DOWN
1. invade
3. abundant
5. eager
6. vigorous
10. persist

1

5th-Grade Vocabulary Success

Keywords

a•bun•dant—uh-BUHN-duhnt *adjective* present in large amounts or numbers
Synonyms: plentiful, full, ample. Antonyms: empty, lacking.

be•stow—bih-STOH *verb* to give or present something to someone
Synonyms: give, grant, award. Antonyms: take, get.

ea•ger—EE-ger *adjective* enthusiastic and impatiently excited
Synonyms: keen, anxious, impatient. Antonyms: indifferent, reluctant.

fra•grant—FRAY-gruhnt *adjective* having a pleasant smell
Synonyms: perfumed, scented, sweet smelling. Antonyms: musty, stinky.

he•ro•ic—hih-ROH-ihk *adjective* 1. showing great bravery, daring, or courage 2. relating to a hero 3. large in size, power, or effect
Synonyms: brave, daring, mighty. Antonyms: cowardly, timid.

in•vade—ihn-VAYD *verb* 1. to enter by force with an army 2. to enter in great numbers or spread over
Synonyms: enter, attack, raid. Antonym: withdraw.

per•sist—per-SIHST *verb* 1. to continue steadily in spite of problems or difficulties 2. to continue to exist
Synonyms: continue, endure, last. Antonyms: discontinue, stop.

spec•ta•cle—SPEHK-tuh-kuhl *noun* a strange or interesting sight
Synonyms: scene, show, wonder. Antonyms: normality, ordinariness.

tri•umph—TRI-uhmf *noun* 1. a great win or achievement 2. a feeling of happiness and pride that comes from success
Synonyms: victory, win, success. Antonyms: loss, defeat.

vig•or•ous—VIHG-er-uhs *adjective* 1. very strong or active, physically or mentally 2. using or displaying great energy or force
Synonyms: active, forceful, energetic. Antonyms: weak, powerless.

Check It!

Page 2
Read & Replace

1. spectacle
2. heroic
3. eager
4. invade
5. fragrant
6. abundant
7. vigorous
8. persist
9. bestow
10. triumph

Page 3
Blank Out!

1. abundant
2. vigorous
3. eager
4. spectacle
5. bestow
6. fragrant
7. persist
8. invade
9. triumph
10. heroic

Page 4
Tic-Tac-Toe

1. stinky, dank, smelly
2. attack, seize, storm
3. extravaganza, marvel, wonder
4. endure, continue, remain

Page 5
Criss Cross

ACROSS
2. fragrant
4. spectacle
7. heroic
8. bestow
9. triumph

DOWN
1. invade
3. abundant
5. eager
6. vigorous
10. persist

Read & Replace

READ the letter. The **bold** words are SYNONYMS to the keywords.
Synonyms are words that have the same meanings, like *big* and *huge*.

FILL IN the blanks with keywords from the word box.

abundant	bestow	eager	fragrant	heroic
invade	persist	spectacle	triumph	vigorous

Dear Jenna,

That was quite a 1 Spectacle **show** you put on today. I had no idea you were capable of such 2 ________ **brave** acts. I can't believe you were so 3 ________ **keen** to rescue us and put yourself in danger. Who could have predicted that a swarm of bees would 4 ________ **attack** our lunch area? They must have been attracted to the 5 ________ **sweet-smelling** flowers, or maybe it was the 6 ________ **plentiful** amounts of perfume Counselor Kim was wearing. When I heard the buzzing sound, I crawled under the picnic table. It was the most 7 ________ **energetic** workout I've had all summer! It's a good thing that you're not allergic to bees. Amber said you had to really 8 ________ **keep going** to get rid of all the bees. The counselors are going to 9 ________ **award** on you the title of Camp Iwannagohome's Bravest Camper!

Congratulations on your 10 ________ **victory**!

Your BFF,
Marcus

Check It!

Page 6

Night & Day

1. c
2. d
3. b
4. h
5. e
6. i
7. j
8. f
9. a
10. g

Page 7

Blank Out!

1. invade
2. vigorous
3. fragrant
4. spectacle
5. abundant
6. bestow
7. eager
8. heroic
9. triumph
10. persist

Page 8

Petal Power

1. eager
2. abundant
3. vigorous
4. heroic

Blank Out!

FILL IN the blanks with keywords.

1. Gail and Shanta always go fishing in April. The fish in Trout Lake are ______________ in spring.
2. If you want to be an Olympic athlete, you will have to go through ______________ training.
3. Evan was ______________ to get to the beach before everyone else, so he woke up early.
4. The Fourth of July fireworks were a real ______________.
5. The coach says he will ______________ the honor of team captain on Dumont next season.
6. The ______________ smell of cinnamon buns made Wendy hungry.
7. Juan was determined to ______________ through the dance-a-thon, even though his feet were aching.
8. Angel spotted an army of ants that was about to ______________ our picnic.
9. Finally jumping her bike over the ramp was a ______________ for Deanna.
10. The firefighter who rescued the little boy did a ______________ deed.

Tic-Tac-Toe

PLAY Tic-tac-toe with synonyms and antonyms. CIRCLE any word that is a synonym to the blue word. PUT an X through any antonyms. Antonyms are words that have opposite meanings, like *happy* and *sad*. When you find three synonyms or antonyms in a row, you are a winner! The line can go across, down, or horizontally.

HINT: If you find a word you don't know, check a dictionary or thesaurus.

Example:

bestow

give	award	take
obtain	grant	get
remove	withhold	present

1. fragrant

musty	perfumy	smelly
aromatic	dank	foul smelling
stinky	scented	sweet smelling

2. invade

withdraw	fall back	attack
raid	retreat	seize
vacate	overrun	storm

3. spectacle

event	normality	show
extravaganza	marvel	wonder
usualness	sight	ordinariness

4. persist

endure	stop	end
discontinue	continue	linger
quit	survive	remain

Criss Cross

FILL IN the grid by writing keywords that are synonyms to the clues.

ACROSS	DOWN
2. ~~Perfumed~~	1. Raid
4. Wonder	3. Ample
7. Mighty	5. Impatient
8. Grant	6. Forceful
9. Success	10. Endure

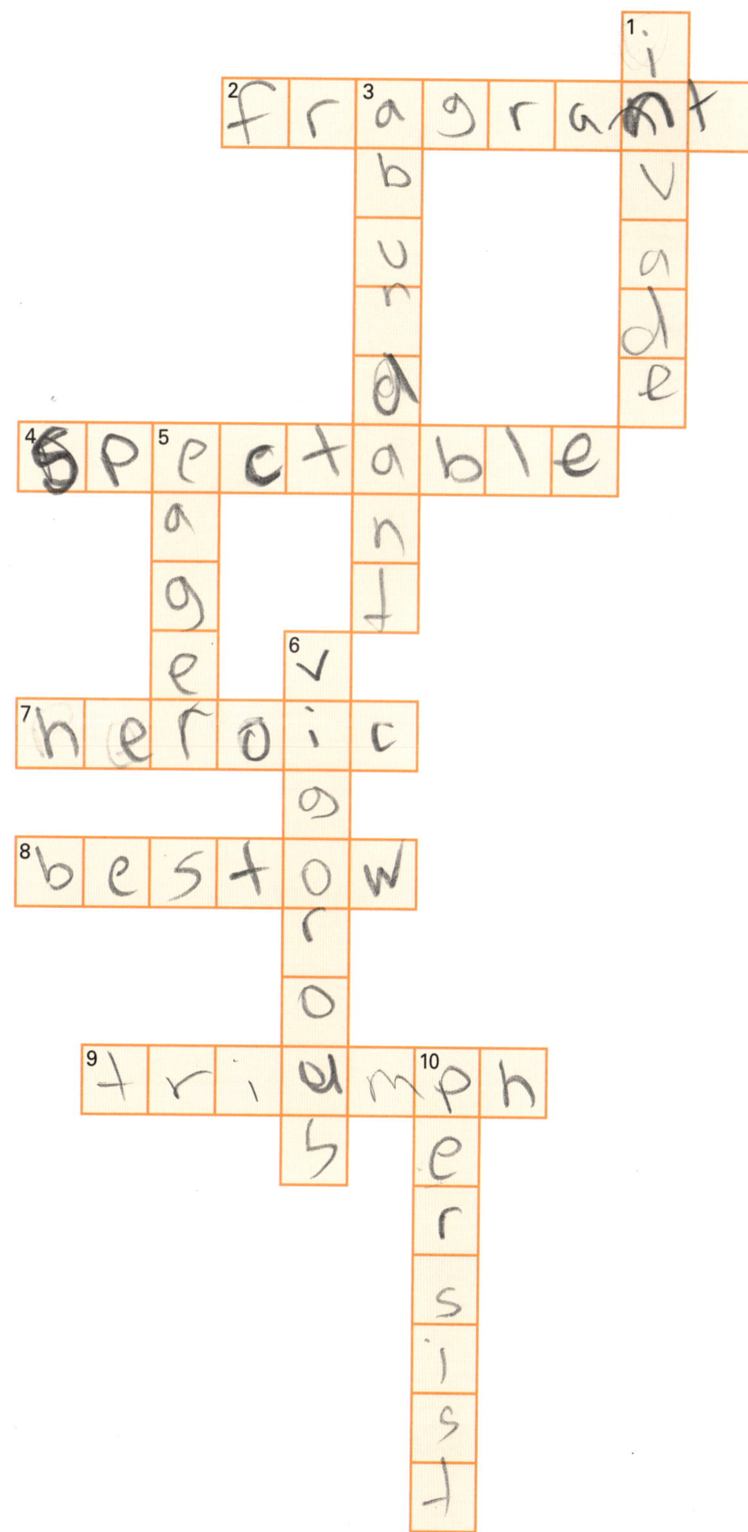

Night & Day

MATCH each word in the moon column to its antonym in the sun column.

HINT: If you don't know the meaning of a word, look it up in a dictionary or thesaurus.

1. eager	______	a. cowardly
2. triumph	______	b. weak
3. vigorous	______	c. reluctant
4. bestow	______	d. defeat
5. persist	______	e. discontinue
6. fragrant	______	f. withdraw
7. spectacle	______	g. empty
8. invade	______	h. take away
9. heroic	______	i. stinky
10. abundant	______	j. normality

Blank Out!

FILL IN each blank with a keyword that is an antonym to the clue underneath.

abundant	bestow	eager	fragrant	heroic
invade	persist	spectacle	triumph	vigorous

1. We watched the crowd ________________ the water park on the hot day.
   leave
2. May was exhausted after her ________________ tennis match against Sue.
   powerless
3. Bees are attracted to the ________________ smell of flowers.
   stinking
4. Lucy said we should all go to the concert tonight. It's supposed to be quite a ________________.
   humdrum event
5. Victor's dad ordered an ________________ supply of pizza for our party.
   empty
6. The mayor will ________________ the key to the city on the winner at the ceremony today.
   get
7. Cassie was ________________ to meet her favorite singer after the concert.
   hesitant
8. Raj's new role-playing video game is filled with ________________ characters.
   timid
9. We're going out to celebrate Ivan's ________________ at the chess competition.
   defeat
10. Kai knew he would ________________ and get to the top of the jungle gym.
    give up

Petal Power

The petals around the flower are ANTONYMS to the word in the center. READ the words around each flower and WRITE an antonym in the center using the keywords.

abundant eager heroic vigorous

Example:

failure
loss triumph defeat
downfall

1.
impatient
indifferent ______ reluctant
hesitant

2.
empty
lacking ______ inadequate
scarce

3.
weak
powerless ______ inactive
sluggish

4.
cowardly
afraid ______ fainthearted
timid

Cut out the Check It! section on page 1, and see if you got the answers right.

Keywords

com•pre•hend—cahm-prih-HEHND *verb* to understand or grasp the meaning of
Synonyms: understand, get, perceive. Antonyms: misunderstand, mistake.

de•vour—dih-VOWR *verb* to eat up quickly and hungrily
Synonyms: gobble, gorge. Antonyms: fast, nibble.

e•merge—ih-MERJ *verb* 1. to come out into view, rise, or appear 2. to become known 3. to come to the end of a difficult or bad experience
Synonyms: rise, show, surface. Antonyms: fade, leave.

fa•tigue—fuh-TEEG *noun* extreme physical or mental tiredness
Synonyms: tiredness, weariness, exhaustion. Antonyms: freshness, energy, vigor.

har•dy—HAR-dee *adjective* 1. strong enough to survive difficult conditions 2. bold and daring
Synonyms: rugged, sturdy, strong. Antonyms: delicate, weak.

in•fe•ri•or—ihn-FEER-ee-er *adjective* 1. less important 2. of lower quality or value
Synonyms: low grade, shabby, lesser. Antonyms: best, superior.

lull—luhl *verb* to soothe or calm
Synonyms: soothe, calm, settle. Antonyms: disturb, alarm.

mis•for•tune—mihs-FAWR-chuhn *noun* 1. bad luck 2. an unpleasant or unhappy event or circumstance
Synonyms: misery, trouble, woe. Antonyms: luck, fortune.

sen•si•tive—SEHN-sih-tihv *adjective* 1. aware of other's needs, problems, and feelings 2. easily hurt or damaged
Synonyms: delicate, tender, touchy. Antonyms: heartless, insensitive.

with•er—WIH*TH*-er *verb* 1. to dry up or shrivel 2. to fade or become weak
Synonyms: droop, fade, shrink. Antonyms: bloom, grow.

Check It!

Page 10

Read & Replace

1. emerge
2. hardy
3. comprehend
4. devour
5. lull
6. sensitive
7. wither
8. fatigue
9. inferior
10. misfortune

Page 11

Petal Power

1. emerge
2. fatigue
3. inferior
4. sensitive
5. wither

Page 12

Blank Out!

1. inferior
2. devour
3. misfortune
4. lull
5. sensitive
6. wither
7. comprehend
8. emerge
9. hardy
10. fatigue

Page 13

Criss Cross

ACROSS
3. sensitive
4. comprehend
7. fatigue
8. hardy
10. misfortune

DOWN
1. emerge
2. wither
5. devour
6. inferior
9. lull

More Synonyms & Antonyms

Read & Replace

READ the e-mail. The **bold** words are SYNONYMS to the keywords. Synonyms are words that have the same meanings, like *happy* and *joyful*. FILL IN the blanks with keywords from the word box.

comprehend	devour	emerge	fatigue	hardy
inferior	lull	misfortune	sensitive	wither

From: Daisy Blossom
To: Meat-Eating Plants R Us
Subject: Tarantuplant

I am writing about the plant seed I ordered. In the beginning, I was very happy with your product. I watched the plant 1 ________ (**surface**) from the soil. It grew and grew and soon appeared quite 2 ________ (**strong**). Unfortunately I did not 3 ________ (**understand**) exactly how strong it would get. "Chewy" quickly began to 4 ________ (**gobble**) everything in her path. It was all I could do to stop her from gobbling up my pets! They squeal and hiss at Chewy all the time. I've tried to 5 ________ (**soothe**) them, but they're still upset. My rattlesnake is very 6 ________ (**delicate**), and now he won't come out from behind his rock! I don't want to see Chewy 7 ________ (**fade**), but I have to lock her in a closet. I'm suffering from 8 ________ (**exhaustion**) trying to find enough food for her. May I please return her? I don't think your product is 9 ________ (**shabby**), but I cannot handle any more 10 ________ (**trouble**).

Check It!

Page 14

Tic-Tac-Toe

1. tender, vulnerable, emotional
2. bloom, blossom, flourish
3. mediocre, shabby, shoddy
4. robust, sturdy, solid

Page 15

Blank Out!

1. wither
2. sensitive
3. emerge
4. hardy
5. lull
6. misfortune
7. comprehend
8. devour
9. inferior
10. Fatigue

Page 16

Night & Day

1. d
2. e
3. h
4. g
5. i
6. b
7. j
8. c
9. f
10. a

Petal Power

The petals around the flower are ANTONYMS to the word in the center. Antonyms are words that have opposite meanings, like *up* and *down*. READ the words around each flower and WRITE an antonym in the center using the keywords.

emerge fatigue inferior sensitive wither

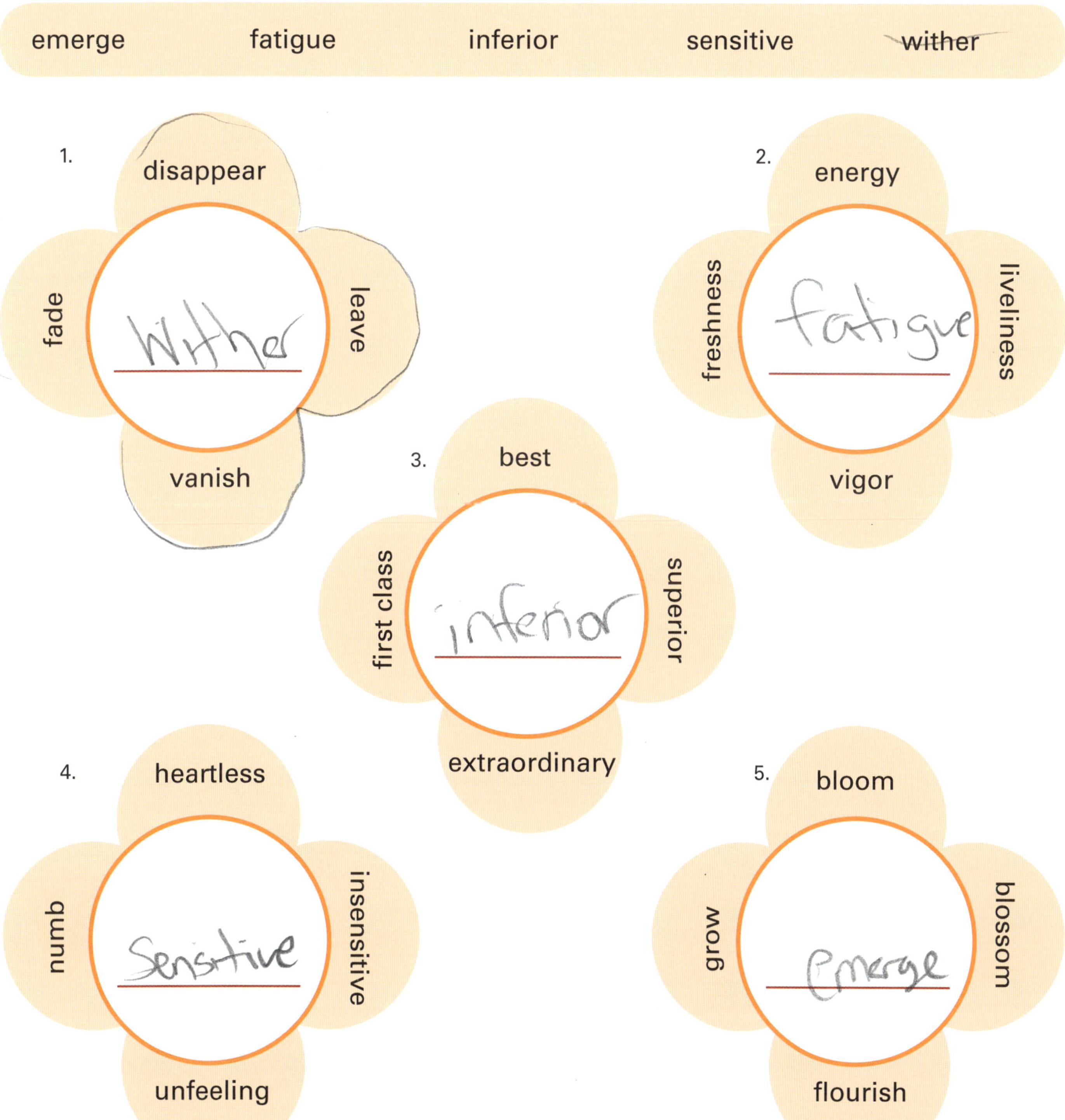

Blank Out!

FILL in the blanks with keywords.

comprehend	devour	emerge	fatigue	hardy
inferior	lull	misfortune	sensitive	wither

1. The DVD was of ____________________ quality, so we returned it to the store.
2. Nat said he could ____________________ a whole chocolate cake by himself.
3. Lynette could not believe her ____________________ when she saw that her worst enemy had joined her cheerleading squad.
4. Baxter tried to ____________________ his baby sister to sleep, but she just kept on screaming.
5. Malik is a good person to talk to because he's so ____________________.
6. The beans will just ____________________ on the vine if we don't pick them soon.
7. Joy couldn't ____________________ why Beth would want to go parasailing on such a rainy day.
8. Carlo watched the butterfly ____________________ from its chrysalis.
9. Princess is a ____________________ dog. She likes to run around outside all day, even when it's freezing cold.
10. A nap might cure your ____________________ .

Criss Cross

FILL IN the grid by writing keywords that are synonyms to the clues.

ACROSS

3. Touchy
4. Perceive
7. Weariness
8. Rugged
10. Woe

DOWN

1. Rise
2. Fade
5. Gorge
6. Lesser
9. Settle

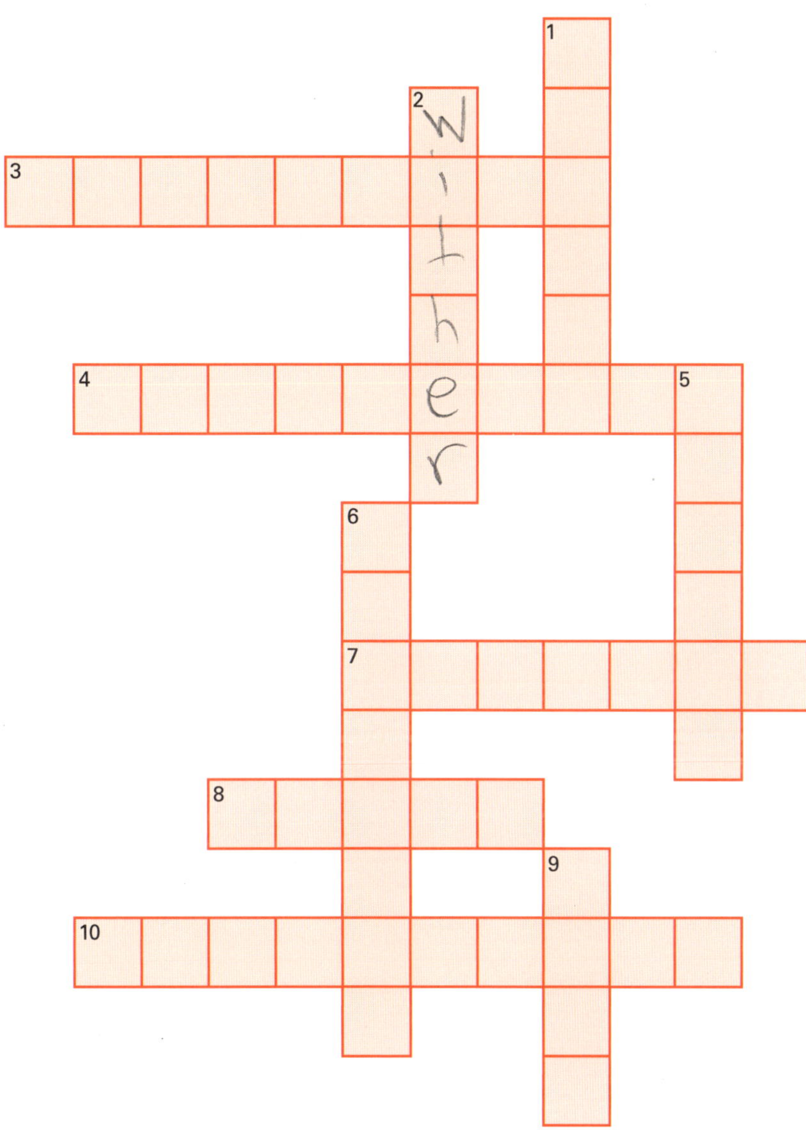

Tic-Tac-Toe

PLAY Tic-tac-toe with synonyms and antonyms. CIRCLE any word that is a synonym to the blue word. PUT an X through any antonyms. When you find three synonyms or antonyms in a row, you are a winner! The line can go across, down, or horizontally.

Example:

emerge

fade	disappear	leave
go away	surface	show
rise	appear	vanish

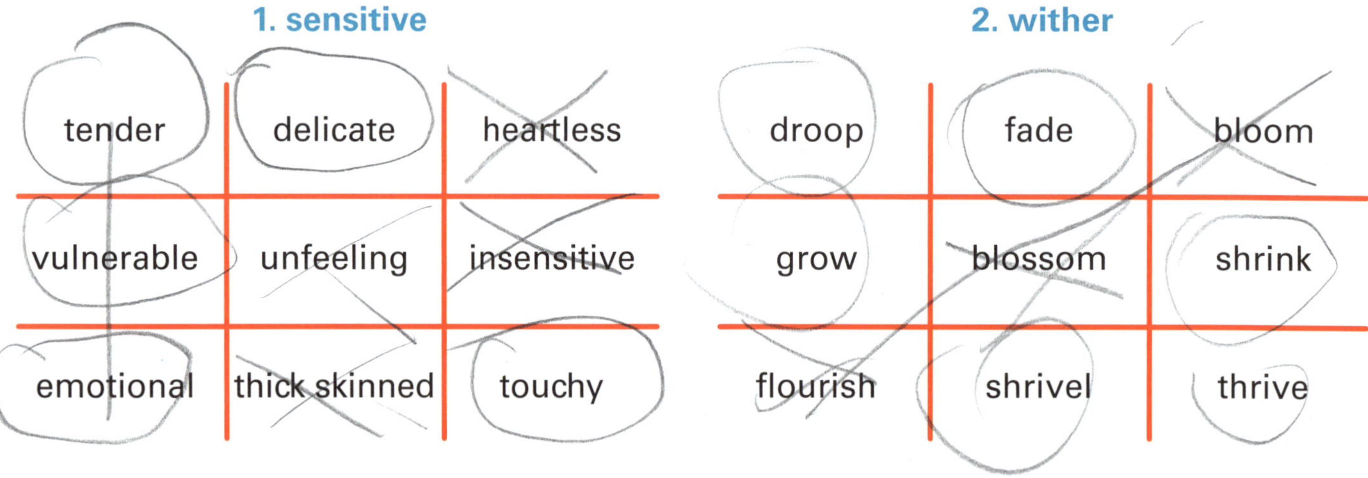

1. sensitive

tender	delicate	heartless
vulnerable	unfeeling	insensitive
emotional	thick skinned	touchy

2. wither

droop	fade	bloom
grow	blossom	shrink
flourish	shrivel	thrive

3. inferior

first class	foremost	best
mediocre	shabby	shoddy
second rate	poor	superior

4. hardy

robust	weak	tough
strong	sturdy	feeble
unhealthy	rugged	solid

Blank Out!

FILL IN each blank with a keyword that is an antonym to the clue underneath.

comprehend	devour	emerge	fatigue	hardy
inferior	lull	misfortune	sensitive	wither

1. The plants in your garden will ________ (flourish) if you leave them out in a frost.
2. If you are ________ (numb) to loud noises, you should move away from the speaker.
3. Kenny's trainer thinks he will ________ (fade) as one of the top runners in our town.
4. Only the most ________ (weak) athletes should sign up for the dogsled competition.
5. The singer tried to ________ (disturb) the crowd so she could start her song.
6. Hans had the ________ (good luck) of watching his lunch get eaten by hungry bears.
7. Yolanda's dad could not ________ (misunderstand) what her text messages meant.
8. The ancient sea monster could ________ (nibble) a shark in one bite.
9. You shouldn't buy that cell phone because it's ________ (superior) to this new one.
10. ________ (Energy) is one of the symptoms of the flu.

Night & Day

MATCH each word in the moon column to its antonym in the sun column.

HINT: If you don't know the meaning of a word, look it up in a dictionary or thesaurus.

1. emerge ______
2. inferior ______

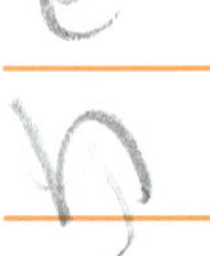

3. devour ______

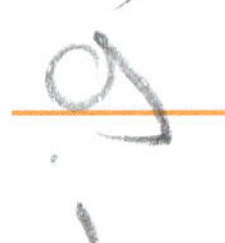

4. lull ______
5. wither ______

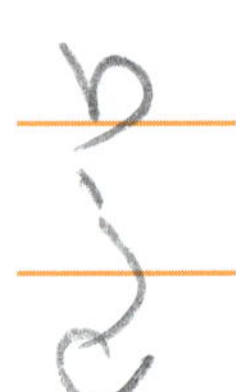

6. comprehend ______
7. fatigue ______
8. sensitive ______

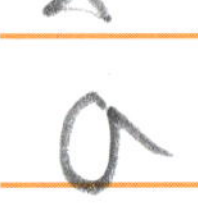

9. misfortune ______
10. hardy ______

a. weak
b. misunderstand
c. heartless
d. fade
e. better
f. luck
g. disturb
h. nibble
i. bloom
j. energy

Check It!

Cut out the Check It! section on page 9, and see if you got the answers right.

Homographs

Keywords

a•lert[1]—uh-LERT *adjective* 1. watchful and ready to face danger or emergency 2. active and brisk

a•lert[2]—uh-LERT *noun* 1. an alarm or warning of danger 2. a time of careful watching and readiness for danger 3. the period of time when an alert is in effect

ape[1]—ayp *noun* a chimpanzee, gorilla, or other tailless mammal in the same family

ape[2]—ayp *verb* to copy or imitate somebody or something

min•ute[1]—MIHN-iht *noun* 1. a period of 60 seconds or one sixtieth of an hour 2. a short period of time

mi•nute[2]—mi-NOOT *adjective* 1. very small 2. of little importance 3. marked by close attention to detail

sub•ject[1]—SUHB-jihkt *noun* 1. one who is under the rule of another 2. something that is being discussed, studied, or written about 3. an area of study

sub•ject[2]—suhb-JEHKT *verb* 1. to make someone go through an unpleasant experience 2. to bring under control 3. to expose to something

vault[1]—vawlt *noun* 1. an arched roof or ceiling 2. a secure room or compartment for keeping valuables 3. a burial chamber

vault[2]—vawlt *verb* to jump quickly or leap over

Check It!

Page 18

Read & Replace

1. alert
2. ape
3. subject
4. minute
5. vault
6. minute
7. subject
8. ape
9. alert
10. vault

Page 19

Homograph Hopscotch

1. minute
2. subject
3. vault

Page 20

Blank Out!

1. alert
2. ape
3. vault
4. ape
5. minute
6. subject
7. alert
8. vault
9. minute
10. subject

Page 21

Double Match Up

1. e, p
2. h, s
3. g, q
4. a, j
5. c, t
6. d, r
7. f, o
8. i, l
9. m, n
10. b, k

Read & Replace

HOMOGRAPHS are words that have the same spelling but different meanings and sometimes different pronunciations. The *train* you ride and how you *train* your dog are homographs.

READ the story. FILL IN the blanks with keywords.

HINT: Read the whole story before you choose your words. Remember, each word has two meanings, so you can use it more than once.

alert	ape	minute	subject	vault

Something wasn't right at the zoo today. I noticed that the lions looked wide-eyed and 1 alert______. They're usually sleepy during the day. My brother and I saw a large furry 2 ape______. The animal thought it was funny to 3 ______ people to flying banana peels. In the distance, I saw a 4 ______ figure slinking around. I took out my binoculars and saw the ape's trainer 5 ______ over the wall. She was only gone for a 6 ______, and then she hopped back in again. I scribbled a note to my brother, and he ran off. The 7 ______ of my note was the suspicious activity of the ape trainer. I realized that I was talking to myself when I saw a little boy 8 ______ my gestures. "Scram!" I yelled. Suddenly the zookeeper blasted a bullhorn as an 9 ______. Soon my brother came by with the police. The trainer had tried to break into a secret 10 ______ underneath the ape house. Mystery solved!

Page 22

Criss Cross

ACROSS
4. subject
5. alert

DOWN
1. minute
2. vault
3. ape

Double Trouble

1. intent
2. stall
3. incline
4. spout
5. impression
6. express

Page 23

Write It Right

1. minute
2. subject
3. vault
4. ape
5. alert

Riddle: silence

Page 24

Blank Out!

1. ape
2. subject
3. minute
4. vault
5. alert
6. vault
7. alert
8. ape
9. minute
10. subject

Homograph Hopscotch

LOOK AT the definitions in each hopscotch board. FILL IN the matching keyword at the top of the board.

1. 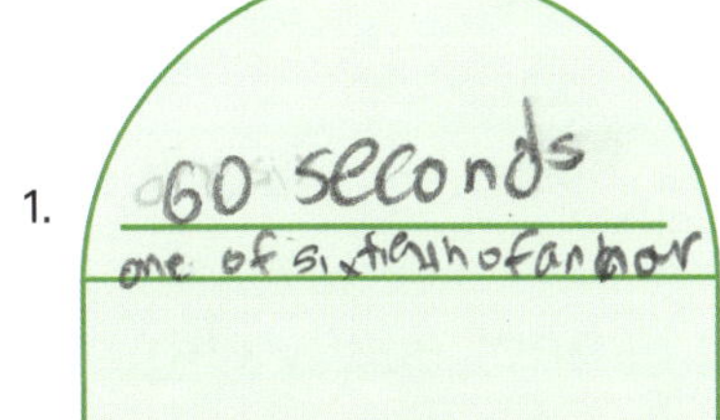

4. 60 seconds

2. very small

3. one sixtieth of an hour

1. of little importance

2. 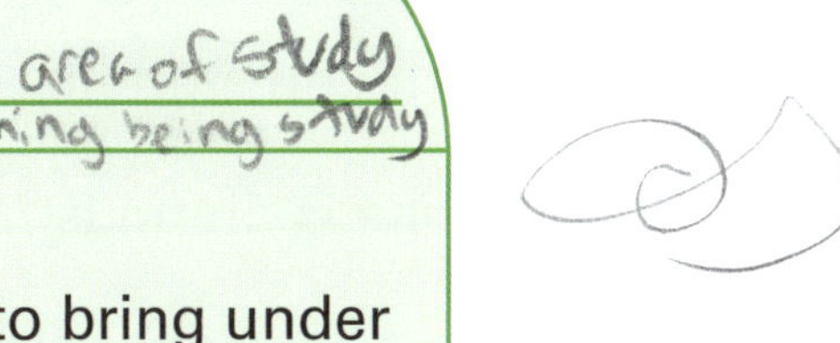

4. to bring under control

2. an area of study

3. to expose to something

1. something being studied

3. 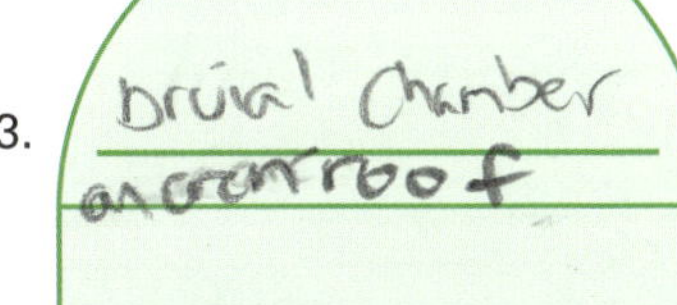

4. to jump quickly

2. an arched roof

3. a burial chamber

1. a secure room for keeping valuables

Blank Out!

FILL in the blanks with keywords.

alert	ape	minute	subject	vault

1. The TV screen started flashing with a tornado ________________.
2. The gorilla is an unusual ________________ because it cannot easily climb trees.
3. Annie put her handheld game system in the hotel ________________ while she went snorkeling.
4. Jack's little sister likes to ________________ every move he makes. It drives him crazy.
5. A ________________ can seem like a long time when you're standing on a stage by yourself.
6. I can't believe Greg's uncle wanted to ________________ us to hours of his favorite polka CDs.
7. The lifeguard will ________________ us if there is a dangerous riptide.
8. Gabby used a pole to ________________ over the high jump bar.
9. This telescope is so powerful we can see ________________ details on the moon.
10. Aliens and space invaders are the ________________ of Hannah Lee's new book.

Double Match Up

FIND the two meanings for each word. Then WRITE the letters of the definitions that match the word.

HINT: If you get stumped, use a dictionary or thesaurus.

1. brace ______ ______
2. carp ______ ______
3. degree ______ ______
4. drain ______ ______
5. gorge ______ ______
6. mean ______ ______
7. lumber ______ ______
8. sheer ______ ______
9. story ______ ______
10. toll ______ ______

a. a pipe that carries water away
b. to ring a bell
c. to eat greedily
d. unkind
e. a support
f. to walk slowly
g. a unit of temperature measurement
h. a large fish
i. a thin fabric
j. to empty
k. a fee charged to use a road
l. straight up or down without a break
m. a short work of fiction
n. one of the levels of a building
o. wood
p. to prepare for something dangerous
q. a qualification given after finishing college or university
r. to have in mind or intend
s. to complain
t. a deep narrow valley

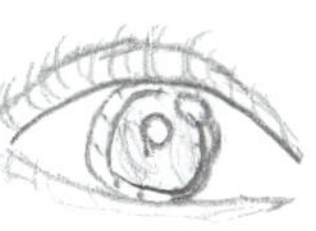

Criss Cross

FILL IN the grid by writing keywords that are synonyms to the clues.

ACROSS

4. An area of study OR to bring under control
5. An alarm OR active and brisk

DOWN

1. A short period of time OR very small
2. To leap over OR a burial chamber
3. To copy OR a member of the chimp family

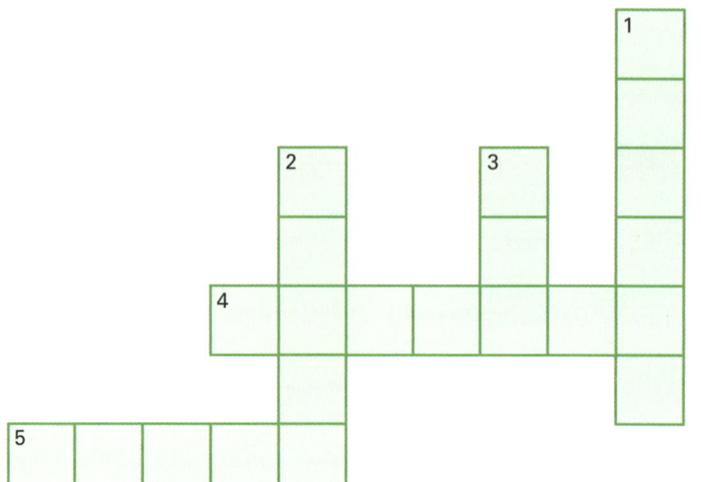

Double Trouble

WRITE the homograph that matches each description.

incline express impression intent spout stall

1. Something planned OR focused on one thing ____________________
2. A booth set up to show goods OR to avoid doing something until later ____________
3. A sloping surface OR likely to think or act in a certain way ____________________
4. The part of a container through which liquids can be poured OR to talk about something at great length ____________________
5. A mark left by pressing something hard into something soft OR a belief about something ____________________
6. To state thoughts or feelings OR traveling quickly ____________________

Write It Right

FILL IN the blanks by answering the clues with keywords. Then UNSCRAMBLE the letters in the circles to answer the riddle.

1. Why don't you stop in for a ___ ◯ ◯ ___ ___ ___ ?
2. Javier liked the acting, but he thought the ◯ ___ ___ ___ ___ ◯ ___ of the movie was boring.
3. We went to see the ___ ___ ___ ◯ ___ where the mummy was buried.
4. An orangutan is a type of ___ ___ ◯ .
5. Hilda's pet cat is most ___ ___ ◯ ___ ___ in the middle of the night.

Riddle

What is so fragile even saying its name can break it? ___ ___ ___ ___ ___ ___ ___

Blank Out!

FILL in the blanks with keywords.

alert	ape	minute	subject	vault

1. I know Justin thinks it's funny to ________________ me, but I don't like it.
2. Zoe was excited to be the ________________ of a newspaper article about kids who recycle.
3. It will only take Bella a ________________ to dry her hair.
4. We can't believe that Tiny is going to try to ________________ over that wall.
5. Did you see the hurricane ________________ on the news?
6. The museum has even more paintings locked in a ________________.
7. Pauline is a great table-tennis player because she's so ________________.
8. The baboon is a monkey, not an ________________.
9. There's a ________________ amount of sugar left in the jar.
10. I hope Mei doesn't ________________ me to her endless questions about my brother.

Check It!

Cut out the Check It! section on page 17, and see if you got the answers right.

Just Right!

You've learned a lot of words so far. Are you ready to have some fun with them?

Synonyms may have similar meanings, but it's important to know which one is the right one to use in different situations. READ each sentence. Then CIRCLE the synonym that best fits the sentence.

1. TJ says she will give / bestow the comic book to me when she's finished.
2. We're waiting for the chick to rise / emerge from the egg.
3. Be careful with the crystal snowflake. It's sensitive / delicate.
4. Our refrigerator is full / abundant of food.
5. The wheels on that skateboard are inferior / low grade to these wheels.

Seesaw

LOOK AT the seesaws. WRITE a synonym on the level seesaws. Write an antonym on the slanted seesaws.

1. eager
2. triumph
3. wither
4. inferior
5. persist
6. hardy

Check It!

Page 25

Just Right!

1. give
2. emerge
3. delicate
4. full
5. inferior

Seesaw

Suggestions:

1. excited
2. loss
3. shrivel
4. superior
5. stop
6. strong

Page 26

Pathfinder

1. inferior, superior
2. lull, alarm
3. fragrant, musty
4. heroic, timid
5. invade, withdraw
6. devour, fast

Page 27

Word Search

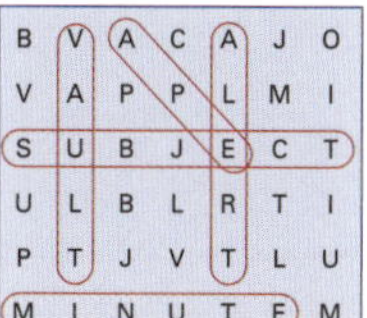

Double Trouble

1. ready to face danger
2. a large tailless mammal
3. 60 seconds
4. an area of study
5. to jump over

Pathfinder

Antonyms are opposites, and knowing your opposites can get you a long way in this game. Begin at START. When you get to a box with arrows leading you to two different boxes, follow the antonym to a new word. If you make all the right choices, you'll end up at FINISH.

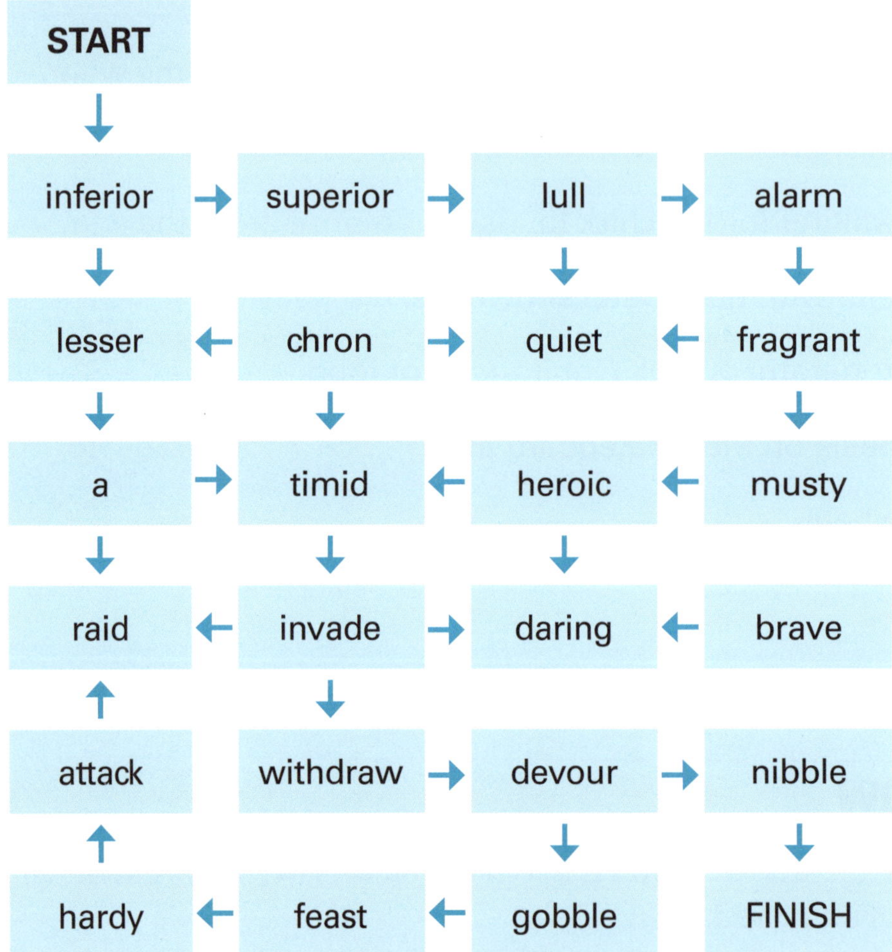

Check It!

Page 28

Sniglets!

1. snowbored
2. instrumeant
3. flopcorn
4. rollerscrape
5. pianope
6. weekdaze

Word Search

CIRCLE the homographs in the word grid. Words go across, up, down, or diagonally.

alert ape minute subject vault

B	V	A	C	A	J	O
V	A	P	P	L	M	I
S	U	B	J	E	C	T
U	L	B	L	R	T	I
P	T	J	V	T	L	U
M	I	N	U	T	E	M

Double Trouble

WRITE another meaning for each keyword.

alert: an alarm OR 1. ____________________

ape: to copy OR 2. ____________________

minute: very small OR 3. ____________________

subject: to bring under control OR 4. ____________________

vault: an arched roof OR 5. ____________________

Sniglets!

Would you like to make up a new word? You can start by making up a *sniglet*. Sniglets are fun-sounding words that use pieces of existing words. Here are some sniglets:

flopcorn—the unpopped kernels at the bottom of the microwave popcorn bag
pianope—refuse to practice the piano
weekdaze—the feeling you get when you can't wait for the weekend to come
snowbored—feeling tired of winter sports
rollerscrape—what you get when you fall off your roller skates
instrumeant—what a song is really about

WRITE a sniglet from the list to complete each sentence.

1. I wish spring would get here already because I'm so ________________.
2. Haley read the song's lyrics to find out the ________________, but they were too confusing.
3. Kevin took the popcorn out of the microwave too soon, so there was a lot of ________________.
4. If you don't wear safety equipment at the skate park, you might get a ________________.
5. Tasha said she was going to ________________ because she wanted to play games instead.
6. Ling's ________________ always starts on Wednesday afternoon.

Cut out the Check It! section on page 25, and see if you got the answers right.

Keywords

a•board—uh-BAWRD *adverb* 1. on, onto, or into a ship or other vehicle 2. in or into an organization or group

a•bol•ish—uh-BAHL-ihsh *verb* 1. to put an end to something 2. to destroy

ab•sent—ab-SUHNT *adjective* 1. not attending or present 2. not existing 3. not paying attention

ab•sorb—uhb-SAWRB *verb* 1. to take in and make part of the whole 2. to soak up or suck in 3. to hold someone's attention

ad•just—uh-JUHST *verb* 1. to make small changes that make something fit or function better 2. to adapt to a new setting or situation

ad•mire—ad-MIR *verb* 1. to like and respect very much 2. to have a high opinion of

ad•ven•ture—ad-VEHN-cher *noun* 1. an unusual or exciting journey or event 2. a task, trip, or project that involves danger and risk

ap•a•thy—AP-uh-thee *noun* a lack of interest, feeling, or emotion

a•shore—uh-SHAWR *adverb* on or to the land from the water

a•typ•i•cal—ay-TIHP-ih-kuhl *adjective* not the usual type or kind

Check It!

Page 30

Match Up

absorb, c
ashore, g
adjust, a
apathy, d
adventure, b
atypical, f
aboard, h
absent, j
admire, i
abolish, e

Page 31

Tic-Tac-Toe

1. side, new, bridge
2. rupt, solve, normal
3. fix, little, ject

abbreviate	admission
abnormal	advance
abridge	advertise
abrupt	advice
absolve	alike
absurd	anew
address	aside
adhere	avoid

Page 32

Read & Replace

1. aboard
2. adventure
3. adjust
4. ashore
5. atypical
6. apathy
7. admire
8. abolish
9. absorb
10. absent

Page 33

Criss Cross

ACROSS	DOWN
1. apathy	2 aboard
4. absorb	3. ashore
7. adventure	4. adjust
8. atypical	5. absent
	6. admire
	9. abolish

Page 34

Blank Out!

1. absent
2. adjust
3. absorb
4. abolish
5. adventure
6. atypical
7. ashore
8. admire
9. apathy
10. aboard

Page 35

It's Puzzling!

1. abhor
2. abstract
3. addition
4. address
5. adopt
6. adrift
7. avert

Page 36

Blank Out!

1. apathy
2. ashore
3. adventure
4. aboard
5. absent
6. admire
7. atypical
8. abolish
9. absorb
10. adjust

Match Up

PREFIXES are groups of letters that come at the beginning of a word. The prefixes "a-" and "ad-" mean *to*, *toward*, or *near*. The prefix "a-" can also mean *not* or *without*. "Ab-" means *away from* or *off*.

MATCH the prefixes in the box to the roots. WRITE each word and then MATCH it to its definition.

HINT: You can use each prefix more than once.

a- ab- ad-

sorb ______ ___
shore ______ ___
just ______ ___
pathy ______ ___
venture ______ ___
typical ______ ___
board ______ ___
sent ______ ___
mire ______ ___
olish ______ ___

Definitions:

a. to adapt to a new setting
b. an exciting journey to a place
c. to soak up
d. without feeling
e. to do away with or end
f. not the usual kind
g. to the land from the water
h. onto a ship
i. to have respect for
j. not present

Tic-Tac-Toe

PLAY Tic-tac-toe with prefixes. CIRCLE any root word that could be used with the prefix in blue. PUT an X through any word that could not be used with the prefix. When you find three X's or O's in a row, you are a winner! The line can go across, down, or diagonally. When you're done, make a list of all the words.

1. a-

turn	side	view
like	new	sell
believe	bridge	void

2. ab-

rupt	dress	topic
solve	sociate	breviate
normal	surd	school

3. ad-

fix	dress	vance
vertise	little	here
vice	mission	ject

Other Words Created with Prefixes

Read & Replace

READ the story. FILL IN the blanks with keywords.

aboard	abolish	absent	absorb	adjust
admire	adventure	apathy	ashore	atypical

Kelly jumped 1 ________________ the sailboat, ready to set off on a thrilling 2 ________________. She was about to 3 ________________ the sails when she saw that her best friend Brian was still 4 ________________. "Are you coming, Brian?" Kelly called.

"Nah, I think I'll just stay here," Brian shrugged.

Brian's answer was 5 ________________. He was usually excited to explore new places. Kelly was surprised by Brian's 6 ________________. Then she remembered that Brian had been in a sailboat that flipped over when he was a little boy.

Kelly took a minute to 7 ________________ all the beautiful boats in the harbor. She knew that a little motivation would help to get rid of, or 8 ________________, Brian's fears of sailing. "Brian, throw me your towel," she said.

"Why?" Brian asked.

"I'm going to need it to 9 ________________ all the water after I go diving in the hidden cove." Brian had attended all of their beach club's dives. He was never 10 ________________ from a dive.

"Get your own towel," Brian joked as he climbed aboard the sailboat.

Criss Cross

FILL IN the grid by answering the clues with keywords.

ACROSS

1. No interest
4. To hold someone's attention
7. A risky trip
8. Not like all the others

DOWN

2. Into a group
3. To the shore
4. To adapt to a new situation
5. Not present
6. To think highly of
9. To destroy

Blank Out!

FILL IN the blanks with keywords.

aboard	abolish	absent	absorb	adjust
admire	adventure	apathy	ashore	atypical

1. Naila was ____________ from dance team practice because she had the flu.
2. If you ____________ the straps on your backpack, it won't feel so heavy.
3. Beth watched her T-shirt ____________ the dye.
4. When Dad found gum under the table, he said he was going to ____________ chewing gum in the house.
5. Logan knew the rafting trip would be an incredible ____________.
6. Victor's cat is ____________. He likes to fetch sticks.
7. Deena found a message in a bottle that had washed ____________.
8. I really ____________ Sylvia's persistence.
9. Brenda's ____________ towards the free candy is unbelievable.
10. Angel and I will have lunch ____________ the ship.

It's Puzzling!

MATCH each prefix to a root word. Then WRITE the words in the blanks.

HINT: You can use the same prefix more than once. If you get stumped, use a dictionary.

a-

ab-

ad-

stract

drift

vert

dress

hor

dition

opt

____

____

____

____

____

____

____

Blank Out!

FILL IN the blanks with keywords.

aboard	abolish	absent	absorb	adjust
admire	adventure	apathy	ashore	atypical

1. When you just don't care one way or the other about the summer heat, it's called

   ____________________.

2. When a crab crawls out of the water, it is going ____________________.

3. It would be an ____________________ to go rock climbing with your friends.

4. If you are carrying your bags onto a ship, you are going ____________________.

5. I was ____________________ from tennis practice because I had too much homework.

6. If you look up to your big brother and want to be just like him, you

   ____________________ him.

7. If you dress differently than all the other kids your age, your sense of fashion

   is ____________________.

8. The cafeteria might stop serving French fries if they decide to ____________________

   junk food from the menu.

9. You can use a sponge to ____________________ the juice you've spilled.

10. If you shift your legs because the movie theater seat is uncomfortable, you

    ____________________ your position.

Keywords

con•cen•trate—KAHN-suhn-trayt *verb* 1. to focus attention or thoughts on one thing 2. to draw or bring things closer together 3. to take water out of

con•front—kuhn-FRUHNT *verb* 1. to face someone or something in challenge, to oppose 2. to cause to meet, to bring face to face with something

con•tem•po•rar•y—kuhn-TEHM-puh-rehr-ee *adjective* 1. happening, living, or existing at the same period of time 2. modern or current

con•ver•sa•tion—kahn-ver-SAY-shun *noun* a casual talk with somebody about feelings, ideas, or opinions

de•fend—dih-FEHND *verb* 1. to protect from harm or danger 2. to represent someone in court 3. to offer support for something or someone

de•part—dih-PAHRT *verb* to leave or go away from

de•press—dih-PREHS *verb* 1. to press down or cause to sink 2. to make someone sad 3. to decrease the value of

ex•hale—ehks-HAYL *verb* to breathe out

ex•port—ihk-SPAWRT *verb* 1. to carry away or remove 2. to send to another place for sale or exchange

ex•press—ihk-SPREHS *verb* 1. to state in words 2. to show thoughts and feelings through gestures, art, or drama

Check It!

Page 38

Read & Replace

1. concentrate
2. export
3. contemporary
4. depress
5. conversation
6. express
7. confront
8. defend
9. depart
10. exhale

Page 39

Petal Power

1. con-
2. de-
3. ex-
4. con-
5. de-
6. ex-

Page 40

Tic-Tac-Toe

1. form, done, dense
2. bug, code, feat
3. try, last, vend

concave, concourse, condense, condone, conform, debate, debug, decode

defeat, deliver, exam, explain, expose, extend, extreme

Page 41

Criss Cross

ACROSS
2. depress
5. contemporary
7. conversation
9. defend
10. exhale

DOWN
1. depart
3. express
4. confront
6. concentrate
8. export

Check It!

Page 42

Blank Out!

1. exhale
2. depress
3. export
4. confront
5. concentrate
6. contemporary
7. depart
8. defend
9. conversation
10. express

Page 43

It's Puzzling!

1. conclusive
2. confuse
3. control
4. convex
5. deforest
6. defuse
7. delay
8. excavate
9. exchange
10. exclusive

Page 44

Blank Out!

1. confront
2. exhale
3. export
4. contemporary
5. depart
6. depress
7. express
8. concentrate
9. conversation
10. defend

Read & Replace

Here are some more prefixes that can help you figure out the meaning of a word. The prefix "con-" means *with* or *together*. "De-" means *away* or *down*. "Ex-" means *out* or *from*.

READ the story. FILL IN the blanks with keywords.

concentrate	confront	contemporary	
conversation	defend	depart	depress
exhale	export	express	

Lena tried to 1 ______________ on her book, but she couldn't pay attention. All she could think about was Sam. They worked together in an 2 ______________ store that shipped boogie boards to other countries. They both loved to read the work of 3 ______________ poets. But they had their first fight, and it was starting to 4 ______________ Lena. She remembered their last 5 ______________. Lena just wanted to 6 ______________ her feelings. She felt like Sam never listened to her and that it was time to 7 ______________ the issue. But Sam got angry. Lena tried to 8 ______________ her position, but that only made things worse. She couldn't believe that Sam would ever 9 ______________ without saying goodbye, but he did. Lena took a deep breath and then began to 10 ______________. Then she picked up the phone and dialed Sam's number.

Petal Power

PREFIXES are added to root words to change or tell more details about the root. When you add the prefix "de-" to the root word *ice*, you make the new word *deice*, which means *to take ice away from*.

READ the word roots around each flower. Then WRITE a prefix that could be added to each root in the flower to make another word.

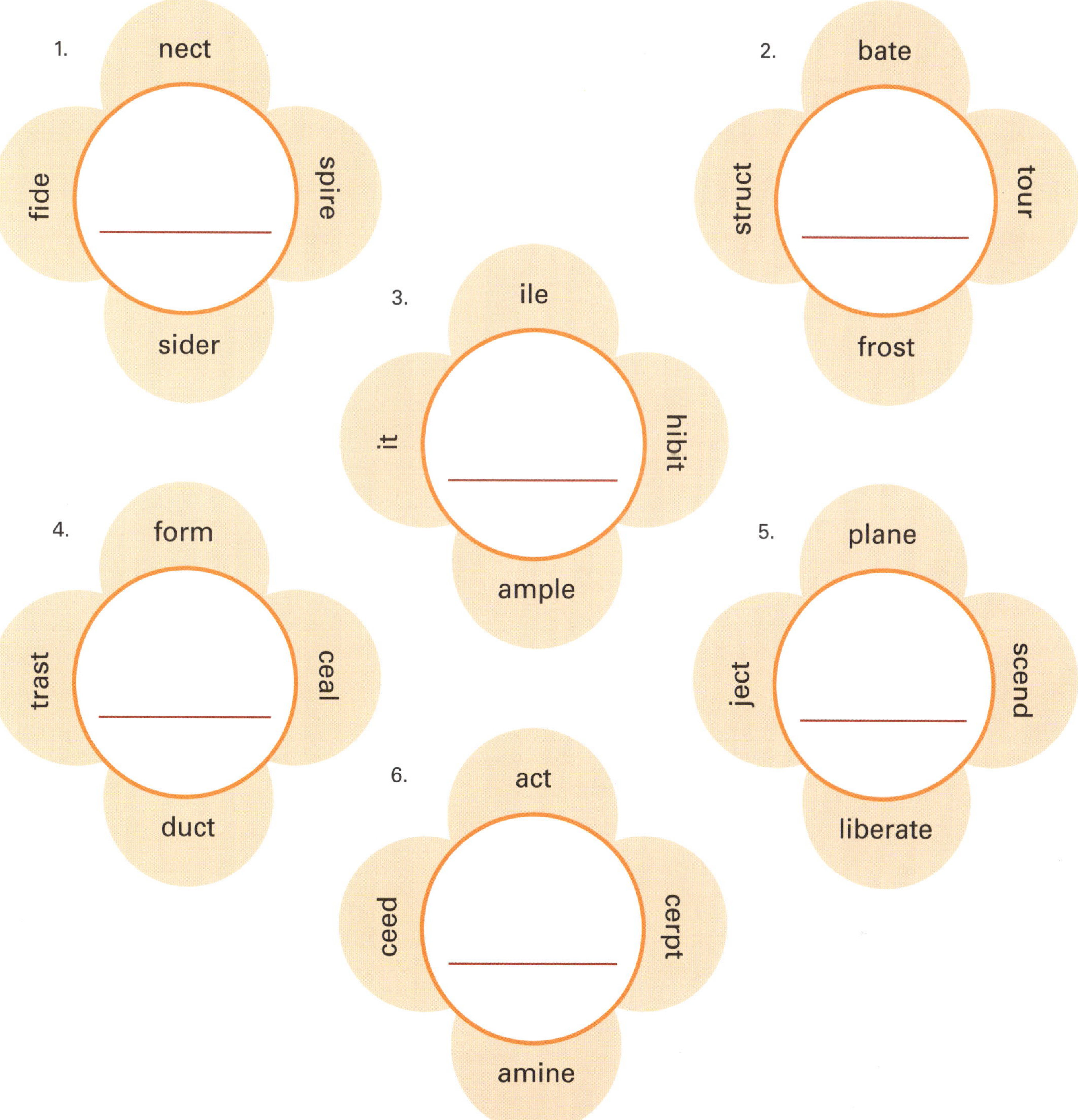

Tic-Tac-Toe

PLAY Tic-tac-toe with prefixes. CIRCLE any root word that could be used with the prefix in blue. PUT an X through any word that could not be used with the prefix. When you find three X's or O's in a row, you are a winner! The line can go across, down, or diagonally. When you're done, make a list of all the words.

1. con-

judge	form	plan
cave	done	act
fell	dense	course

2. de-

bug	mind	bate
code	stand	found
feat	liver	win

3. ex-

try	plain	am
duct	last	tend
pose	treme	vend

Other Words Created with Prefixes

Criss Cross

FILL IN the grid by answering the clues with keywords.

HINT: Use the prefix meanings as a guide.

Prefix Meanings: con- = with, together de- = away, down ex- = out, from

ACROSS

2. Press **down**
5. Living **within** the same time period
7. A talk **with** someone
9. To drive danger **away**
10. To breathe **out**

DOWN

1. To go **away** from
3. To get your feelings **out** in words
4. To go face to face **with** someone
6. To draw things **together**
8. To remove **from**

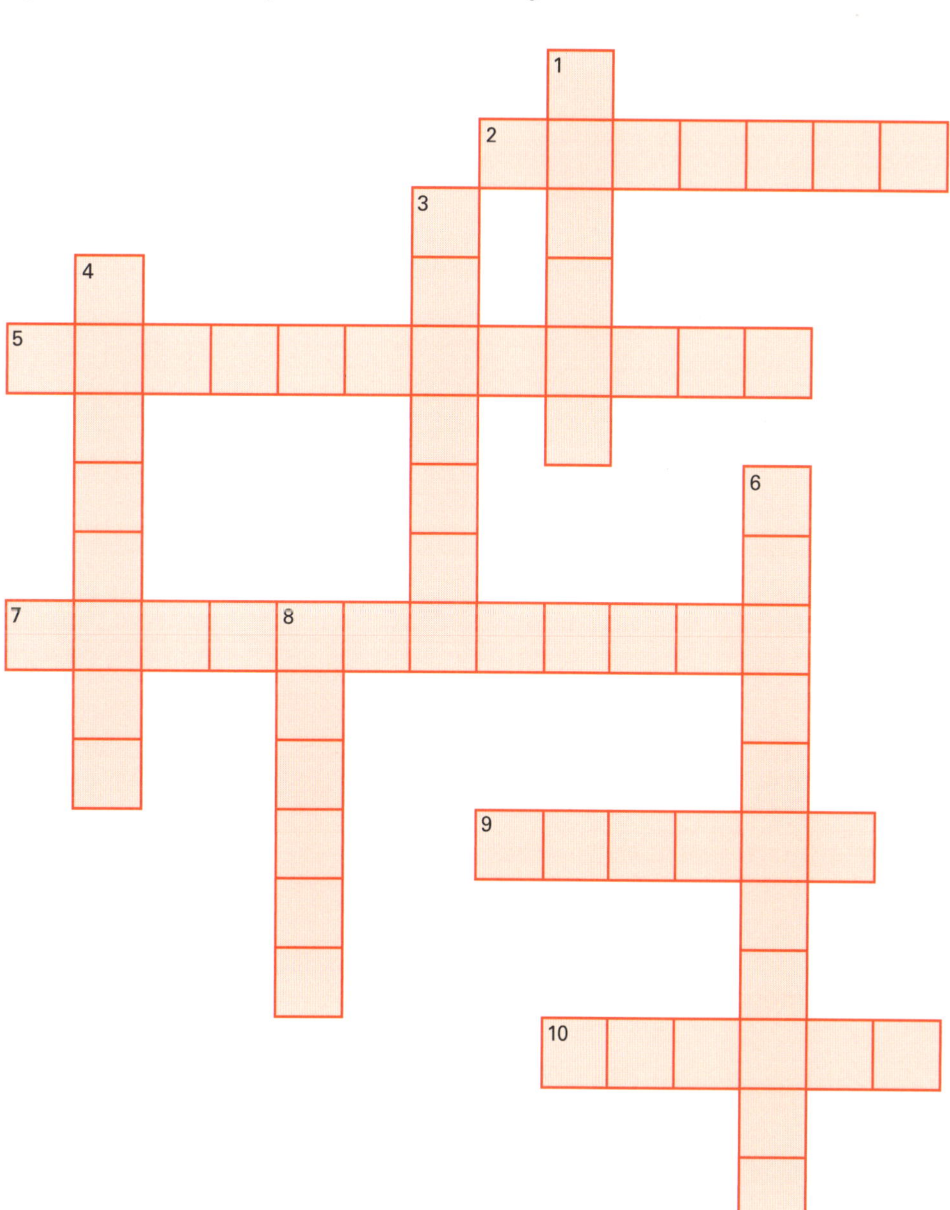

Blank Out!

FILL IN the blanks with keywords.

concentrate	confront	contemporary	conversation	defend
depart	depress	exhale	export	express

1. Jamie could hold her breath for a whole minute before she had to ______________.
2. You need to ______________ the lever to get the toy out of the machine.
3. Hawaiian companies ______________ surfboards to countries all over the world.
4. Kel knew he had to ______________ the bully that was bothering his sister.
5. Hilda found it difficult to ______________ on her routine with all the noise in the auditorium.
6. Matthew checked out the ______________ fiction section to find a book by a current author.
7. The bus will ______________ for the amusement park at 7 a.m.
8. Courtney will have to ______________ her position during the debate.
9. Jalen and his mom were so absorbed in their ______________ they didn't realize it was nearly midnight.
10. Sophia writes song lyrics to ______________ her feelings.

It's Puzzling!

MATCH each prefix to a root word. Then WRITE the words in the blanks.

HINT: You can use the same prefix more than once. If you get stumped, use a dictionary.

con-

de-

ex-

lay

vex

cavate

fuse

trol

clusive

change

forest

Blank Out!

FILL IN the blanks with keywords.

concentrate	confront	contemporary	conversation	defend
depart	depress	exhale	export	express

1. If you want to tell your dad why you're angry, you need to ______________________ him.
2. You have to ______________________ to blow up a balloon.
3. You might need to ______________________ your file onto a CD if you work on your friend's computer.
4. Mogul is a ______________________ style of skiing.
5. Will you wave goodbye when you ______________________ for summer camp?
6. You shouldn't watch a sad movie if it's going to ______________________ you.
7. You can use your smile to ______________________ happiness without saying any words.
8. If you ______________________ on the 3-D picture, you might see something surprising.
9. You can have a ______________________ in person, on the phone, or by text message.
10. If your friend had a reason for being late, you might ______________________ him.

Keywords

ex•tra•cur•ric•u•lar—ehk-struh-kuh-RIHK-yuh-ler *adjective* activities that are outside the regular school or work routine

ex•traor•di•nar•y—ihk-STRAWR-dn-ehr-ee *adjective* better or beyond what is typical or regular, extremely good or special

ex•trav•a•gant—ihk-STRAV-uh-guhnt *adjective* 1. beyond what is reasonable or necessary 2. spending or costing an extremely large amount of money

o•ver•flow—oh-ver-FLOH *verb* to flood or flow over the brim or edge

o•ver•take—oh-ver-TAYK *verb* 1. to catch up with and pass by 2. to catch by surprise

o•ver•whelm—oh-ver-HWEHLM *verb* 1. to take over by greater strength, force, or numbers 2. to overpower in thought or feeling 3. to give a large or excessive amount of something to someone

su•per•in•ten•dent—soo-per-ihn-TEHN-duhnt *noun* 1. a person who manages the way work is done by a group or organization 2. a person who is responsible for taking care of a building

su•pe•ri•or—suh-PEER-ee-er *adjective* 1. better, above average 2. greater in quantity or number 3. higher in rank or importance

su•per•sti•tion—soo-per-STIHSH-uhn *noun* a belief in something that is not real or possible

su•per•vise—SOO-per-viz *verb* to watch over and make sure that a task or activity is being done correctly

Check It!

Page 46

Read & Replace

1. extracurricular
2. overwhelm
3. superintendent
4. extraordinary
5. extravagant
6. overflow
7. superstition
8. supervise
9. superior
10. overtake

Page 47

Stack Up

EXTRA: terrestrial, galactic, sensory
OVER: grown, cast, joyed
SUPER: market, nova, hero

Page 48

Tic-Tac-Toe

1. active, board, look
2. bent, vect, look
3. hero, sonic, flow

extramural
extravaganza
extrovert
overachieve
overactive
overboard
overcome
overeat
overlook
supercenter
superfine
superhighway
superhuman

Page 49

Criss Cross

ACROSS
1. supervise
5. extracurricular
6. overflow
7. overtake
8. superior

DOWN
2. extravagant
3. extraordinary
4 superintendent
7. overwhelm

Read & Replace

READ the letter. FILL IN the blanks with keywords.

extracurricular	extraordinary	extravagant	overflow
overtake	overwhelm	superintendent	superior
superstition	supervise		

Dear Mr. Askalot,

We received your petition for a new 1 ________________ activity for students who meet after school. The 100,000 names on your list really did 2 ________________ me, so I shared your petition with my 3 ________________. Unfortunately, while we agree that a kayak run would be an 4 ________________ activity, the cost of creating a river would be 5 ________________. There is also the danger that during a storm, the river would 6 ________________. Some people here believe the wacky 7 ________________ that kayaks bring bad luck. Please submit a new proposal. I can 8 ________________ the program's development. Many believe our neighboring town, Bestville, is 9 ________________ to our town, and a great program might help us 10 ________________ their position of number 1 on the "Best Places to Live If You Need a Great After-School Program" list.

Sincerely,
Ms. Humdrum

✓ Check It!

Page 50

Blank Out!

1. extravagant
2. overwhelm
3. superstition
4. extracurricular
5. supervise
6. extraordinary
7. overflow
8. superior
9. superintendent
10. overtake

Page 51

It's Puzzling!

1. extracellular
2. extraneous
3. overcharged
4. oversleep
5. overstep
6. overworked
7. supercharged
8. superimpose
9. supertanker

Page 52

Blank Out!

1. superstition
2. overtake
3. supervise
4. extravagant
5. extracurricular
6. overwhelm
7. superintendent
8. overflow
9. superior
10. extraordinary

Stack Up

LOOK AT the root words in the box. MATCH them with prefixes to make new words.

WRITE the new words under each prefix.

Prefix Meanings: *extra- = outside* *over- = too much* *super- = more, better, higher*

market	terrestrial	grown	galactic	nova
sensory	hero	cast	joyed	

extra-

____

____

____

over-

____

____

____

super-

____

____

____

Tic-Tac-Toe

PLAY Tic-tac-toe with prefixes. CIRCLE any root word that could be used with the prefix in blue. PUT an X through any word that could not be used with the prefix. When you find three X's or O's in a row, you are a winner! The line can go across, down, or diagonally. When you're done, make a list of all the words. HINT: If you're not sure about some of the words, use a dictionary.

1. over-

achieve	call	active
come	cept	board
end	eat	look

2. super-

fine	dict	center
bent	vect	look
highway	human	flow

3. extra-/extro-

hero	sonic	flow
duct	vert	vaganza
mural	mand	ject

Other Words Created with Prefixes

Criss Cross

FILL IN the grid by answering the clues with keywords.

ACROSS

1. To make sure a task is being done correctly
5. Outside the regular school or work day
6. To flow over the brim
7. To catch by surprise
8. Higher in rank or importance

DOWN

2. Costing an extremely large amount of money
3. Extremely special
4. A person who takes care of a building
7. To overpower in thought or feeling

Blank Out!

FILL IN the blanks with keywords.

extracurricular	extraordinary	extravagant	overflow	overtake
overwhelm	superintendent	superior	superstition	supervise

1. Rita's motorized scooter was an ________________ present.
2. We're planning to ________________ the other team with our powerful front line.
3. Zoe believes the ________________ that four-leaf clovers are lucky.
4. Karate is Justin's favorite ________________ activity.
5. Mr. Garcia asked Marisol to ________________ the beach cleanup.
6. Amir has the ________________ ability to pick up his guitar and play any song that he's heard.
7. Clark shouted when he saw the pool ________________ into the yard.
8. Lin uses the expert trail because she is a ________________ skier.
9. Brendan helped the building ________________ shovel a path after the snowstorm.
10. If our team gets two more wins, we'll ________________ the Bulldogs in the standings.

It's Puzzling!

MATCH each prefix to a root word. Then WRITE the words in the blanks.

HINT: You can use the same prefix or root more than once. If you get stumped, use a dictionary.

extra-

over-

super-

worked

impose

step

neous

cellular

tanker

sleep

charged

____

____

____

____

____

____

____

____

____

Blank Out!

FILL IN the blanks with keywords.

extracurricular	extraordinary	extravagant	overflow	overtake
overwhelm	superintendent	superior	superstition	supervise

1. If you think the number 13 is bad luck, you believe in a ____________________.

2. If you pass by the other runners on the track, you ____________________ them.

3. When you babysit your little brother, you have to ____________________ him.

4. Inviting 1,000 friends to your birthday party would be ____________________.

5. All the activities you do outside of school are ____________________.

6. If you swim in the ocean, a large wave could ____________________ you.

7. The ____________________ in your school makes sure the air conditioning is working on a hot day.

8. If you pour juice into a glass and it spills over the top, you have made it ____________________.

9. The ice cream at Frosty's is so delicious. It is definitely ____________________ to the one you buy in a store.

10. Snow in Death Valley is an ____________________ event. It's one of the hottest places on Earth.

Keywords

clar•i•fy—KLAR-uh-fi *verb* 1. to make clear or pure 2. to make understandable

com•put•er•ize—kuhm-PYOO-tuh-riz *verb* to organize, control, or produce something using a computer

dis•in•te•grate—dihs-IHN-tih-grayt *verb* 1. to break into small parts, pieces, or elements 2. to destroy the unity or wholeness of something

em•pha•size—EM-fuh-siz *verb* to give importance or draw special attention to something

fas•ci•nate—FAS-uh-NAYT *verb* to hold someone's interest or attention completely

in•i•ti•ate—ih-NIHSH-ee-ayt *verb* 1. to cause or start something to happen 2. to introduce someone to a new activity, skill, or area 3. to make someone a member of a group, organization, or religion through a special ceremony

le•gal•ize—LEE-guh-liz *verb* to make legal by making or changing a law

mod•i•fy—MAHD-uh-fi *verb* 1. to change slightly 2. to make less severe or extreme

nav•i•gate—NAV-ih-gayt *verb* 1. to find a course to follow and steer a vehicle there 2. to travel to water 3. to make one's way over or through

pu•ri•fy—PYUR-uh-fi *verb* 1. to remove harmful or unwanted substances to make something pure 2. to grow or become pure or clean

Check It!

Page 54

Read & Replace

1. modify
2. computerize
3. emphasize
4. fascinate
5. clarify
6. navigate
7. purify
8. disintegrate
9. legalize
10. initiate

Page 55

Suffix Hopscotch

1. -fy/-ify
2. -ate
3. -ize

Page 56

Match Up

1. beautify
2. itemize
3. alphabetize
4. falsify
5. hydrate
6. alienate

Page 57

Criss Cross

ACROSS	DOWN
4. modify	1. clarify
7. disintegrate	2. emphasize
8. initiate	3. computerize
9. purify	5. fascinate
10. navigate	6. legalize

Read & Replace

A SUFFIX comes at the end of a word and has its own meaning. READ the letter. FILL IN the blanks with keywords.

clarify	computerize	disintegrate	emphasize	fascinate
initiate	legalize	modify	navigate	purify

Suffix Meanings: *-fy = make, do* *-ize = make, become* *-ate = make, cause*

Dear Editor,

I saw that you are going to 1 ________ your magazine. It looks like you will 2 ________ everything and publish a digital magazine. I want to 3 ________ that there are paper lovers left. I know it's hard to believe that paper could 4 ________ anyone, but it is true. Let me 5 ________ my feelings. I find it difficult to 6 ________ through the World Wide Web. My garage is full of old issues of *Rock, Scissors, Paper Illustrated.* I have designed a system to 7 ________ the air so paper will not 8 ________ over time. I am also working to 9 ________ collecting magazines from other people's trash because it is against the law. I understand that you had reasons to 10 ________ this process.

I hope you'll reconsider your decision.

Your Loyal Reader,
P.T. Pulp

Page 58

Blank Out!

1. modify
2. navigate
3. disintegrate
4. emphasize
5. purify
6. computerize
7. fascinate
8. clarify
9. initiate
10. legalize

Page 59

Chopping Block

1. real
2. solid
3. captive
4. simple
5. class
6. accessory
7. active
8. type
9. civil
10. different

Page 60

Blank Out!

1. clarify
2. purify
3. computerize
4. emphasize
5. initiate
6. modify
7. legalize
8. disintegrate
9. navigate
10. fascinate

Suffix Hopscotch

LOOK AT the roots in each hopscotch board. FILL IN a suffix that can be added to all of the words in the board.

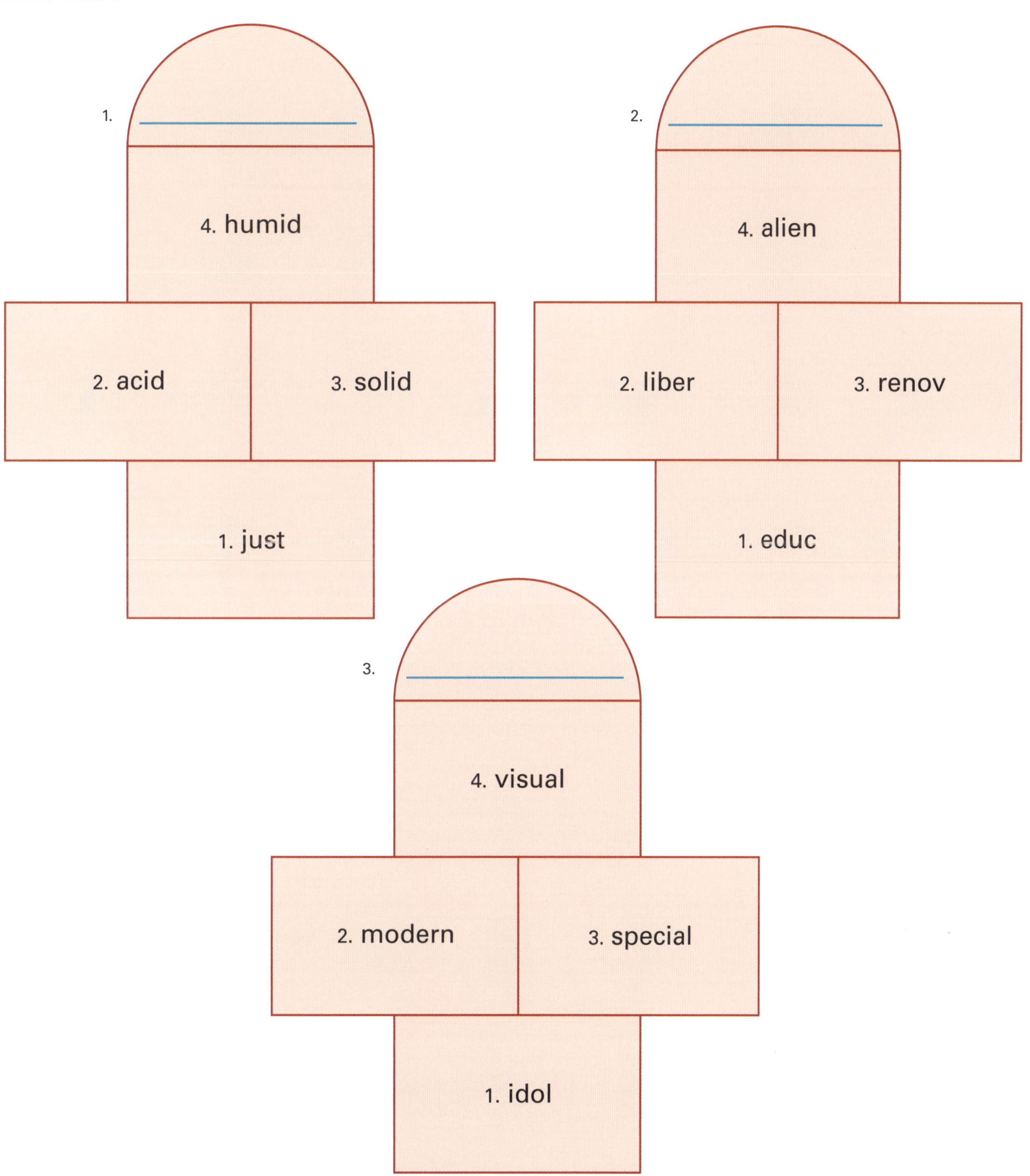

Match Up

MATCH each root to a suffix. Then WRITE the word next to its definition.

HINT: Sometimes you drop or change a letter from the root word when you add the suffix.

Root	Suffix
alphabet	-ate
alien	-ize
beauty	-fy
hydr	-ate
false	-ize
item	-fy

	Word	Definitions
1.	______________________	to make beautiful
2.	______________________	to make a list of details
3.	______________________	to put in alphabetical order
4.	______________________	to make false
5.	______________________	to supply with fluid or moisture
6.	______________________	to make unfriendly

Criss Cross

FILL IN the grid by answering the clues with keywords.

ACROSS

4. To make less extreme
7. To cause to break into small pieces
8. To make someone a member of a group
9. To become clean
10. To make a course and follow

DOWN

1. To make clear
2. To draw attention to
3. To produce with a computer
5. To hold someone's attention completely
6 To make legal

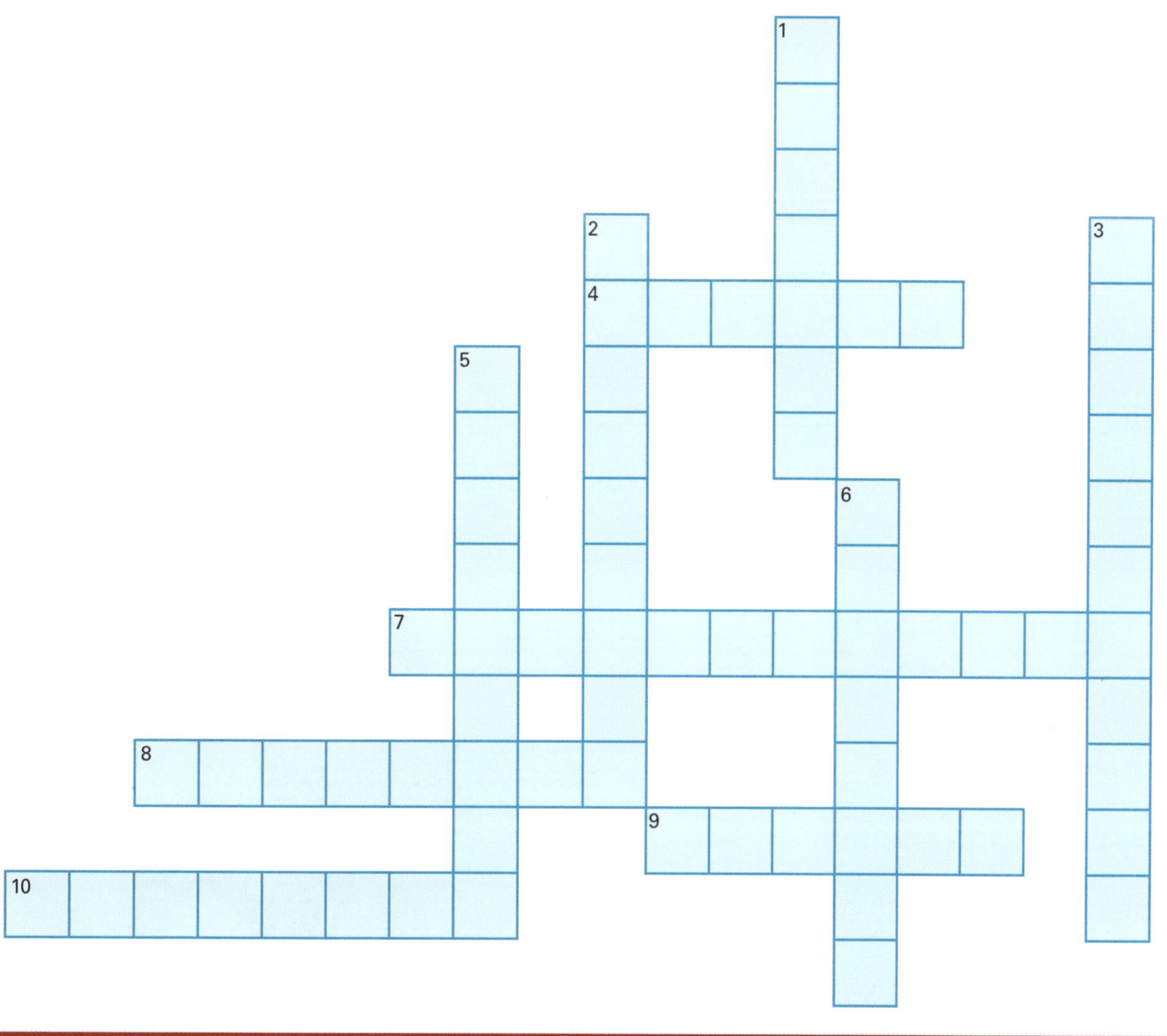

Blank Out!

FILL IN the blanks with keywords.

clarify	computerize	disintegrate	emphasize	fascinate
initiate	legalize	modify	navigate	purify

1. The coach showed Judith how to ____________________ her pitch so she could throw faster.
2. Vera and Leo brought maps to help them ____________________ through the woods.
3. Sonia's group of friends started to ____________________ as soon as she changed schools.
4. Keiko used a highlighter to ____________________ the important words in her letter.
5. Adriana brought a filter on her trip so she could ____________________ the drinking water.
6. Paul helped his mom ____________________ all the files in her office.
7. Donna didn't understand why the circus seemed to ____________________ so many people.
8. Dan asked his trainer to ____________________ the meaning of her instructions.
9. Our club is hoping to ____________________ a new recycling program.
10. Violet disagreed with her town's decision to ____________________ gambling.

Chopping Block

READ the words. CHOP OFF the suffix in each word by drawing a line right before the ending. WRITE the root word in the blank.

HINT: You may have to change or add a letter or two to make the root word.

1. realize ______
2. solidify ______
3. captivate ______
4. simplify ______
5. classify ______
6. accessorize ______
7. activate ______
8. typify ______
9. civilize ______
10. differentiate ______

Blank Out!

FILL IN the blanks with keywords.

clarify	computerize	disintegrate	emphasize	fascinate
initiate	legalize	modify	navigate	purify

1. If you don't understand what someone is saying, you need him to ____________________ it.
2. You can get a machine that will take dirt out of the air and ____________________ it.
3. When you use your laptop to keep track of your schedule, you ____________________ it.
4. If you slam your hand down while you speak, you want to ____________________ what you are saying.
5. Some clubs like to ____________________ new members at a special celebration.
6. If you put a new seat and handlebar on your bike, you ____________________ it.
7. If you think people under 18 should be able to vote, you want them to ____________________ teen voting.
8. When you sit by a campfire, you can watch the burning wood ____________________.
9. Astronauts use computers to ____________________ through outer space.
10. If your friend says a book is so good you won't be able to put it down, he means it will ____________________ you.

Keywords

am•bas•sa•dor—am-BAS-uh-der *noun* 1. an important official sent to represent a country in a foreign place 2. someone who serves as an official representative of something

an•ces•tor—AN-sehs-ter *noun* someone from the past to whom a person is directly related, usually more distant than a grandparent

at•ten•dant—uh-TEHN-duhnt *noun* someone whose job it is to serve or help people

bi•ol•o•gist—bi-AHL-uh-jihst *noun* a scientist who studies living things

con•fi•dant—KAHN-fih-dahnt *noun* a person who is trusted with secrets

im•mi•grant—IHM-ih-gruhnt *noun* someone who has left his country to go live in another country

op•er•a•tor—AHP-uh-ray-ter *noun* a person whose job it is to run or control a machine

pac•i•fist—PAS-uh-fihst *noun* someone who is against fighting and wars

pe•des•tri•an—puh-DEHS-tree-uhn *noun* someone who travels by walking

phy•si•cian—fih-ZIHSH-uhn *noun* a doctor, someone who is qualified to practice medicine

Check It!

Page 62

Read & Replace

1. confidant
2. ancestor
3. pacifist
4. immigrant
5. ambassador
6. biologist
7. physician
8. pedestrian
9. attendant
10. operator

Page 63

Suffix Hopscotch

1. –ian
2. –ist
3. -ant

Page 64

What Do I Do?

1. pedestrian
2. confidant
3. ambassador
4. immigrant
5. operator
6. biologist
7. pacifist
8. attendant
9. physician
10. ancestor

Page 65

Criss Cross

ACROSS
1. pedestrian
3. physician
5. ambassador
6. pacifist
7. attendant
8. biologist

DOWN
2. immigrant
4. confidant
5. ancestor

Read & Replace

READ the story. FILL IN the blanks with keywords.

ambassador	ancestor	attendant	biologist	confidant
immigrant	operator	pacifist	pedestrian	physician

Suffix Meanings: -ant, -ian, -ist = one who

Dear Diary,

You are my only 1 ____________. I can't tell anyone else what I want to be when I grow up. There's so much pressure when you have an 2 ____________ who was the queen of Ancientia. She was a famous 3 ____________ who kept her nation out of war. My grandmother was the first 4 ____________ to move to the United States from her town. She worked hard and was eventually made the 5 ____________ to her homeland. Then there's my uncle, a famous 6 ____________ who discovered a new species of butterfly. And my older brother, a doctor, is the President's 7 ____________! I don't want to be any of those things. I'd like to be a crossing guard and just help a 8 ____________ cross the street safely. Or maybe a locker room 9 ____________ who brings water and towels to the athletes. I'd even be happy as the 10 ____________ of the cotton candy machine at the circus.

Thanks for listening,
Connie T. Ented

Check It!

Page 66

Blank Out!

1. physician
2. immigrant
3. ambassador
4. attendant
5. pacifist
6. ancestor
7. biologist
8. confidant
9. operator
10. pedestrian

Page 67

Chopping Block

1. serve
2. violin
3. account
4. mathematics
5. guard
6. tour
7. Egypt
8. natural
9. type
10. occupy

Page 68

Blank Out!

1. physician
2. pacifist
3. ambassador
4. pedestrian
5. attendant
6. ancestor
7. biologist
8. confidant
9. immigrant
10. operator

Suffix Hopscotch

LOOK AT the roots in each hopscotch board. FILL IN a suffix that can be added to all of the words in the board. HINT: You may have to change a letter of the root word.

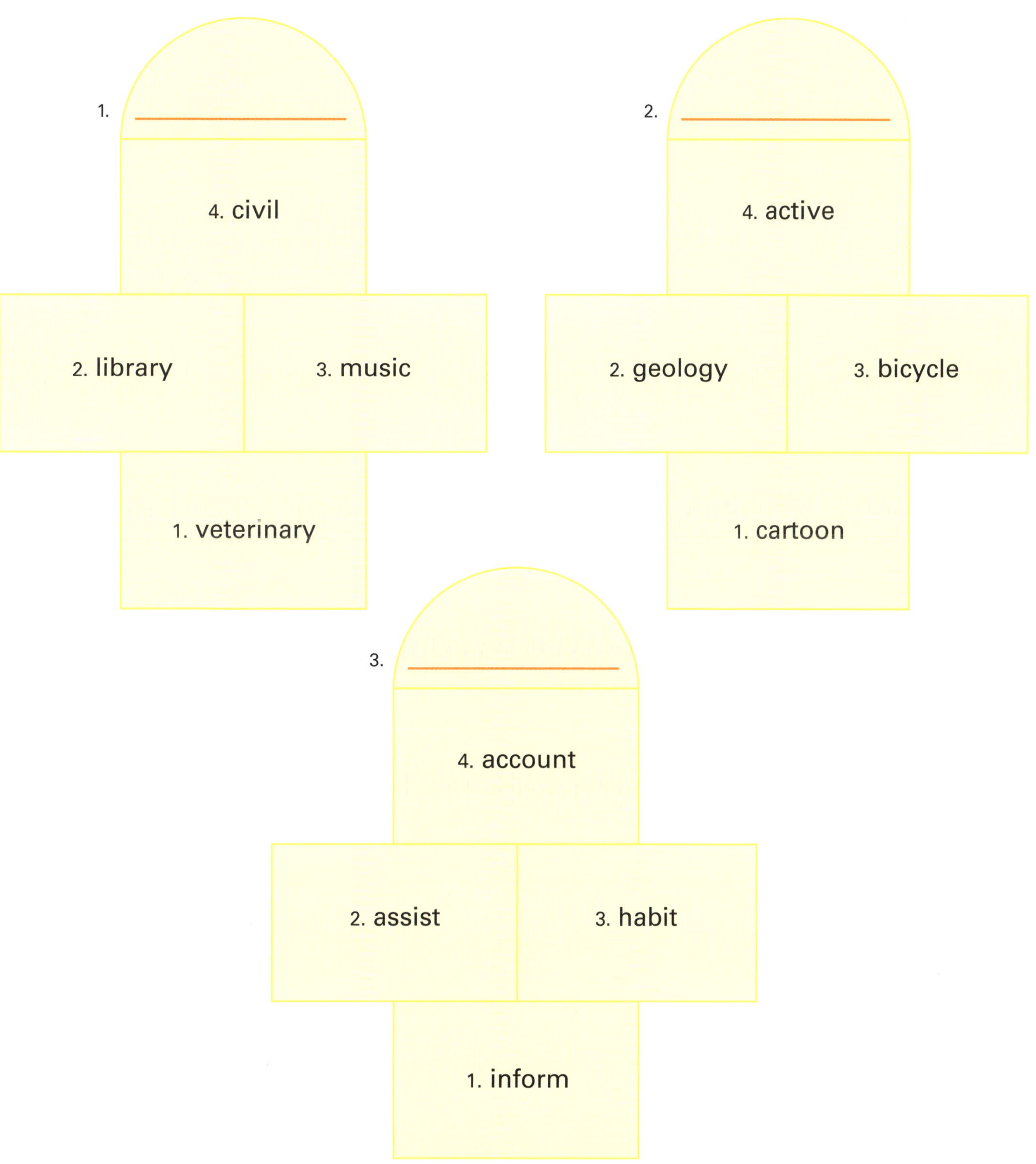

What Do I Do?

MATCH each key word to a description. Then WRITE the word on the card.

ambassador	ancestor	attendant	biologist	confidant
immigrant	operator	pacifist	pedestrian	physician

1. I walk around town.

   ____

2. You can tell me your secrets.

   ____

3. I officially represent my home country.

   ____

4. I left my country to live here.

   ____

5. I control a big machine.

   ____

6. I study living things.

   ____

7. I believe war is wrong.

   ____

8. I serve people at the gas station.

   ____

9. I can make you feel better when you're sick.

   ____

10. I'm your grandmother's grandmother's grandmother.

    ____

Criss Cross

FILL IN the grid by answering the clues with keywords.

ACROSS

1. One who walks
3. One who practices medicine
5. One who represents a country
6. One who is against violence
7. One who serves or helps
8. One who studies living things

DOWN

2. One who went to live in a new country
4. One who hears secrets
5. One who someone is descended from

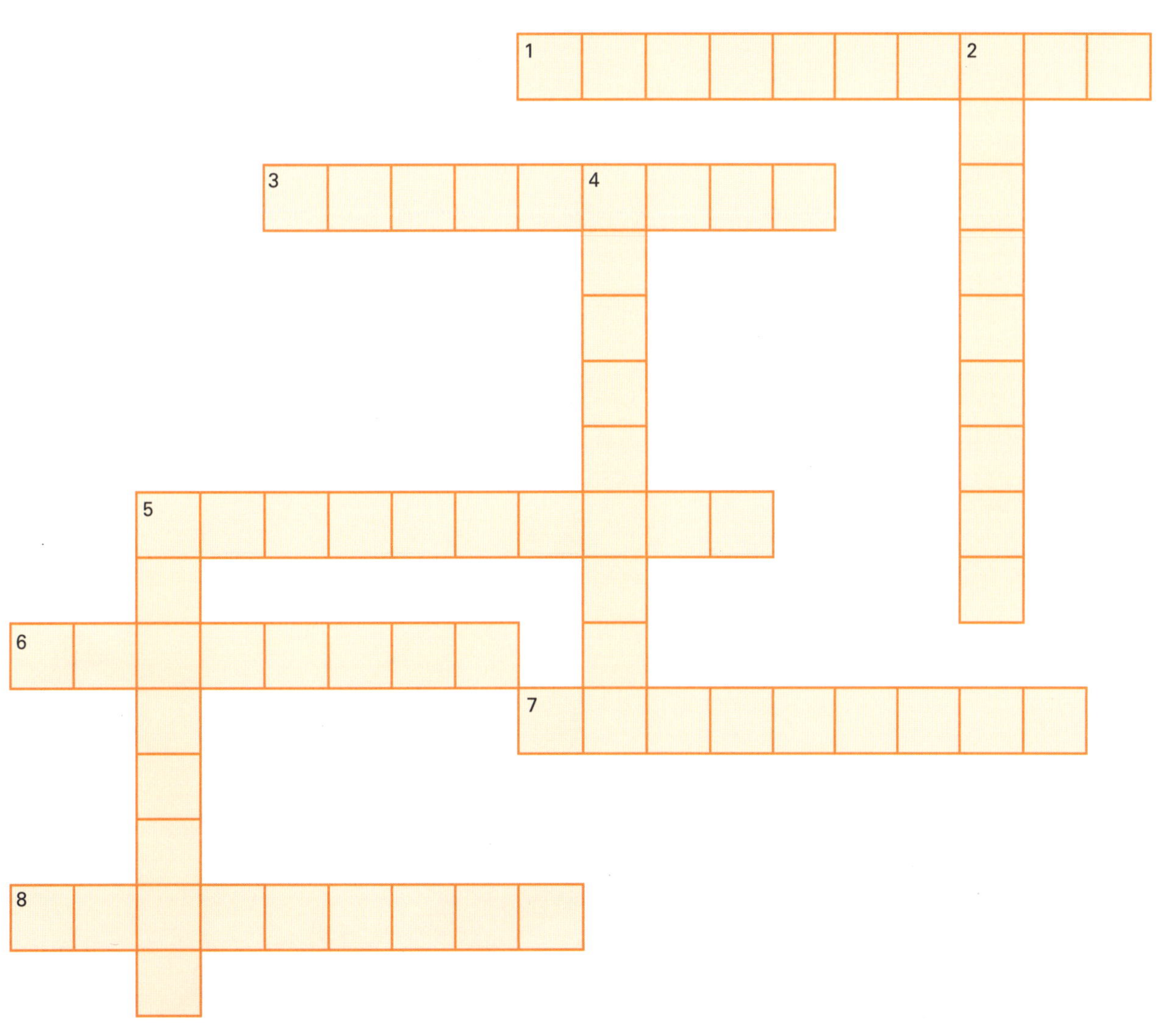

Blank Out!

FILL IN the blanks with keywords.

ambassador	ancestor	attendant	biologist	confidant
immigrant	operator	pacifist	pedestrian	physician

1. Byron saw the team ____________________ after he twisted his ankle.
2. Igor and his parents are going to leave Russia to live here. He is an ____________________.
3. Ife's mother is the Nigerian ____________________. She works at the embassy.
4. Nicole got a summer job working as a pool ____________________.
5. David's sister is a ____________________. She believes it is wrong to fight.
6. Connor treasured the war medallion that belonged to his ____________________.
7. Amy loves plants, trees, and animals. Maybe she will be a ____________________.
8. Martin told Olivia all of his secret hopes and fears. She was his ____________________.
9. My dad's company is looking for an ____________________ who knows how to control a crane.
10. Our town is planning a new ____________________ lane for the bridge.

Chopping Block

READ the words. CHOP OFF the suffix in each word by drawing a line right before the ending. WRITE the root word in the blank.

HINT: You may have to change or add a letter or two to make the root word.

1. servant ______________________
2. violinist ______________________
3. accountant ______________________
4. mathematician ______________________
5. guardian ______________________
6. tourist ______________________
7. Egyptian ______________________
8. naturalist ______________________
9. typist ______________________
10. occupant ______________________

Blank Out!

FILL IN the blanks with keywords.

ambassador	ancestor	attendant	biologist	confidant
immigrant	operator	pacifist	pedestrian	physician

1. You need to see a ____________________ when you are sick.
2. You are a ____________________ if you believe you should figure out disagreements by talking rather than fighting.
3. If you need help in a foreign country, you can talk to our country's ____________________.
4. When you walk around town instead of driving, you are a ____________________.
5. The gas station ____________________ filled up our car.
6. Someone who lived a long time ago and is related to you is your ____________________.
7. The ____________________ studied bats and other cave-dwelling animals.
8. If you have a ____________________, it should be someone you trust to keep your secrets.
9. If your grandmother was born in a different country and moved away to live here, she's an ____________________.
10. It might be fun to work as the ____________________ of an ice-cream machine.

Pick the One!

Think you've got your prefixes straight? It's time to check your skills. LOOK AT each group of words. CIRCLE the real word in each row.

1. aboard	aport	amire
2. conpart	confront	conhale
3. debolish	detake	depart
4. extratypical	extraordinary	extraflow
5. superior	supersent	superwhelm
6. overshore	overwhelm	overcurricular
7. export	exfend	exshore
8. adventure	adordinary	adpathy
9. abfend	absorb	abjust

Combo Mambo

WRITE all the words can you make by adding the prefixes to the root words.

a- ab- ad- con- de- ex- over- super-

1. press ____________________
2. sent ____________________
3. board ____________________
4. part ____________________

Check It!

Page 69

Pick the One!

1. aboard
2. confront
3. depart
4. extraordinary
5. superior
6. overwhelm
7. export
8. adventure
9. absorb

Combo Mambo

1. depress, express
2. absent, consent
3. aboard, overboard
4. apart, depart

Page 70

Pick the One!

1. operator
2. modify
3. fascinate
4. emphasize
5. pacifist
6. confidant
7. pedestrian
8. physician
9. navigate
10. purify
11 biologist
12. clarify
13. ambassador
14. disintegrate
15. ancestor

Page 71

Pathfinder

1. vise, super
2. attend, ant
3. press, de
4. legal, ize
5. take, over
6. computer, ize

Page 72

Sniglets!

1. maximonkey
2. unfare
3. exaspirin
4. magnifire
5. supersnore
6. minimunch

Pick the One!

Now it's time to test your knowledge of suffixes. You know the rules—just CIRCLE the real word in each row. Ready, set, go!

1.	operatize	operatist	operator
2.	modist	modify	modize
3.	fascinian	fascinize	fascinate
4.	emphasify	emphasor	emphasize
5.	pacifize	pacifist	pacifor
6.	confidian	confidor	confidant
7.	pedestrian	pedestrior	pedestriate
8.	physicor	physisant	physician
9.	navigate	navigatist	navigatize
10.	purate	purant	purify
11.	biologor	biologize	biologist
12.	clarify	clarize	clarate
13.	ambassadant	ambassador	ambassadist
14.	disintegran	disintegrist	disintegrate
15.	ancestor	ancestist	ancestate

Pathfinder

Think you know your prefixes and suffixes pretty well? Then you'll have no problem with this game. Begin at START. When you get to a box with arrows leading you to two different boxes, pick the prefix or suffix that you can add to the root word. If you make all the right choices, you'll end up at FINISH.

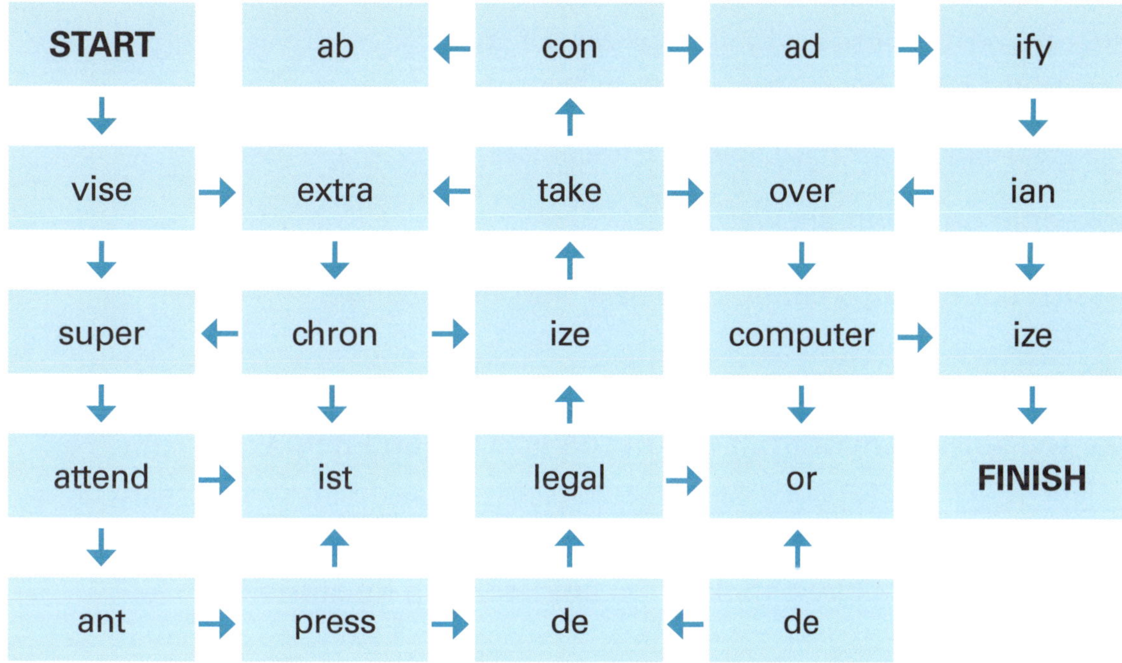

Sniglets!

Are you ready for some more sniglet fun? Here are sniglets made with prefixes and suffixes.

exaspirin—the impossible-to-remove cap on the pill bottle
magnifire—when you start something burning with a magnifying glass
maximonkey—the largest number of monkeys allowed at a zoo
minimunch—the least amount of food you can eat
supersnore—a snore that is so loud you wake yourself up
unfare—when the bus driver charges you too much

WRITE a sniglet from the list to complete each sentence.

1. The zookeeper said that six was the ____________________.
2. When Garth counted his change, he saw that the bus fee was ____________________.
3. Amy wanted something for her toothache and needed help with the ____________________.
4. Raj was trying to get a close look at the spider when he started the ____________________.
5. Julia couldn't get back to sleep after her ____________________.
6. Dad said that one bowl of cereal is the breakfast ____________________.

BONUS!

Now it's your turn. Here are some prefixes and suffixes you can use to create more sniglets.

WRITE DOWN your sniglets and their definitions.

Prefixes
ambi- = both
circum- = around
endo- = within
ultra- = beyond

Suffixes
-oid = form, resembling
-itis = disease
-kinesis = movement
-ship = state of being

____

____

____

____

Roots 9

Keywords

mag•nan•i•mous—mag-NAN-uh-muhs *adjective* showing kindness, generosity, or forgiveness towards someone

mag•nate—mag-NAYT *noun* a person who has earned a lot of wealth and power in a particular industry

mag•nif•i•cent—mag-NIHF-ih-suhnt *adjective* extremely good, beautiful, impressive, or fine

mag•ni•fy—MAG-nuh-fi *verb* 1. to make something appear larger than it is 2. to increase the size, effect, loudness, or intensity of something 3. to make something appear more important than it actually is

mag•ni•tude—MAG-nih-tood *noun* 1. great size, volume, or scale 2. the importance or significance of something

min•i•a•ture—MIHN-ee-uh-cher *adjective* smaller in size or scale than others of its type

min•i•mal—MIHN-uh-muhl *adjective* 1. very small or slight 2. the smallest or least possible

min•i•mize—MIHN-uh-miz *verb* 1. to reduce or keep to the lowest possible amount or degree 2. to intentionally underestimate the seriousness or extent of something

min•i•mum—MIHN-uh-muhm *noun* the lowest or smallest possible amount or degree of something 2. the lowest degree or amount recorded or allowed by law

mi•nor•i•ty—muh-NAWR-ih-tee *noun* less than half of a larger group

Check It!

Page 74
Read & Replace

1. magnanimous
2. magnate
3. minority
4. magnify
5. minimum
6. minimal
7. magnitude
8. minimize
9. magnificent
10. miniature

Page 75
Root It Out

1. magnify
2. minimum
3. magnanimous
4. minority
5. minimize
6. magnate
7. miniature
8. magnificent
9. minimal
10. magnitude

Page 76
Combo Mambo

1. magnification: the act of making something appear larger than it is
2. magnum: a large bottle holding about 1.5 liters
3. minus: less, without
4. minor: smaller or less in importance, size, or degree
5. minimalist: a person whose work displays simplicity
6. magnificence: impressive beauty or greatness

Page 77
Criss Cross

ACROSS

1. minimum
3. magnanimous
4. minimize
6. magnate
8. minority
9. magnitude

DOWN

1. minimal
2. magnificent
5. magnify
7. miniature

Read & Replace

ROOTS can be found at the beginning, middle, or end of a word. Each root has its own meaning. The root *magn* at the beginning of the word *magnificent* means *great*. The root *min* at the end of the word *miniature* means *small*. READ the story. FILL IN the blanks with keywords.

magnanimous	magnate	magnificent	magnify
magnitude	miniature	minimal	minimize
minimum	minority		

Judy looked at the secret potion. She thought it was 1 ____________ of her best friend to let her take the first sip. Andy's mother was a 2 ____________ in the technology industry. Cool, young people were in the 3 ____________ in her office, so she was always bringing home new inventions for Andy to test. The bottle was covered with crystals that seemed to 4 ____________ the liquid inside so it looked like there was an enormous amount in the tiny container. Judy read the label. It said, "Take a 5 ____________ five drops of this potion. Although we have observed 6 ____________ side effects, we do not know the 7 ____________ of this product's effectiveness." Judy dropped five drops of potion onto her tongue. She held her nose to 8 ____________ its bitter taste. At first, Judy felt 9 ____________. She was full of energy and power. Then she looked up. Andy looked like a giant. Judy realized that the potion had turned her into a 10 ____________ version of herself!

Check It!

Page 78

Blank Out!

1. miniature
2. magnificent
3. minority
4. magnanimous
5. minimal
6. minimum
7. magnate
8. magnify
9. magnitude
10. minimize

Page 79

It's Puzzling!

1. diminutive
2. magnanimity
3. minute
4. magnitudinous

Page 80

Blank Out!

1. minority
2. magnify
3. minimize
4. magnate
5. miniature
6. magnanimous
7. minimum
8. magnificent
9. minimal
10. magnitude

Root It Out

LOOK AT each definition. FILL IN the missing root letters.

HINT: The **bold** words give you a clue about the root.

Root meanings: magn = great, large min = small, less

1. If you __________ify a bug, you make it look **larger** than it actually is.
2. The **lowest** speed allowed by law is the __________imum speed limit.
3. You are being __________animous when you show a **great** amount of kindness towards someone.
4. If **less** than half of your class plays guitar, then guitar players are in the __________ority.
5. You can __________imize your trading card collection and make it **smaller** by only keeping the cards that are really valuable.
6. If you've earned a **large** fortune selling ice cream, you are an ice-cream __________ate.
7. If you put **small** marshmallows in your hot cocoa, they are __________iature.
8. A __________ificent painting is one that has **great** beauty.
9. A very **slight** scrape is a __________imal injury.
10. The **great** size of an earthquake is its __________itude.

Combo Mambo

MATCH a word or ending in an orange box to a root in a yellow box to make a word. WRITE the word in the root box. Then LOOK UP the definition for each word and WRITE it in a sentence.

Root meanings: *magn = great, large* *min = small, less*

ification	um	us	or	imalist	ificence

MAGN	MIN
______	______
______	______
______	______

Criss Cross

FILL IN the grid by answering the clues with keywords.

ACROSS

1. The lowest possible amount of something
3. Showing generosity towards another
4. To intentionally underestimate the seriousness of something
6. A person who has a lot of power in an industry
8. Less than half of a larger group
9. The importance of something

DOWN

1. The smallest or least possible
2. Very impressive
5. To make something appear more important than it is
7. Smaller in scale than normal

Blank Out!

FILL IN the blanks with keywords.

magnanimous	magnate	magnificent	magnify	magnitude
miniature	minimal	minimize	minimum	minority

1. Devan builds ____________________ furniture for her dollhouse.
2. We saw a ____________________ fireworks display after the parade.
3. Kids who dislike pizza are in the ____________________ in our class.
4. It was very ____________________ of Trevor to give the last cookie to his sister.
5. The theater requests ____________________ noise once the movie begins.
6. Sixteen is the ____________________ driving age in our town.
7. Amir's father started off with just one ship. Now he is a shipping ____________________.
8. Patricia's telescope can ____________________ the surface of the moon.
9. We didn't realize the play was going to be a production of this ____________________.
10. When Oscar goes water-skiing, he wears a helmet to ____________________ the risk of getting hurt.

It's Puzzling!

MATCH a prefix, root, and suffix together to form a new word. Then WRITE the words in the blanks.

HINT: You can use the same root or suffix more than once, and some words don't have a prefix at all. If you get stumped, use a dictionary.

Prefixes	Roots	Suffixes
di-	magn	-animity
	min	-ute
		-itud
		-inous
		-utive

____

____

____

____

Blank Out!

FILL IN the blanks with keywords.

magnanimous	magnate	magnificent	magnify	magnitude
miniature	minimal	minimize	minimum	minority

1. If you're the only one in your group of friends who wants to go skiing, you're in the ____________________.
2. When you make a problem seem bigger than it is, you ____________________ it.
3. If you ____________________ the amount of time you spend getting dressed in the morning, you can wake up a little later.
4. If you own popular lemonade stands across the country, you could be called a lemonade ____________________.
5. ____________________ horses are half the size of an average horse.
6. If your dad decides to forgive you for coming home late, he is being ____________________.
7. Most roller coasters have a ____________________ height requirement, and if you're shorter, they won't let you on.
8. Cody did a ____________________ jump in the half pipe. It looked like he could touch the clouds.
9. If your room isn't too messy, it will take a ____________________ amount of effort to clean it up.
10. If you think it's not a big deal to lie to your parents, you don't understand the ____________________ of what you've done.

Keywords

con•ces•sion—kuhn-SESH-un *noun* 1. the act of yielding or giving into someone or something 2. a special right or privilege given to someone

e•vac•u•ate—ih-VAK-yoo-ayt *verb* 1. to remove from danger 2. to empty

in•ter•cede—ihn-ter-SEED *verb* to come between two people or groups in order to settle a disagreement

pro•ceed—pruh-SEED *verb* 1. to go on or continue to do something 2. to move in a particular direction

re•cede—rih-SEED *verb* 1. to move away from or go back from a certain point or level 2. to grow less or smaller

se•cede—sih-SEED *verb* to separate or withdraw from an organization, including a country

va•cant—VAY-kuhnt *adjective* 1. not being used, lived in, or occupied 2. showing no signs of thought or expression

va•cate—VAY-kayt *verb* to leave, give up, or withdraw

va•ca•tion—vay-KAY-shuhn *noun* 1. a period of time for rest, travel, and recreation 2. a scheduled period when schools and businesses are closed

vac•u•um—VA-kyoo-uhm *noun* 1. a space that is empty of all matter 2. a device or machine that creates or uses a vacuum

Check It!

Page 82

Read & Replace

1. evacuate
2. vacant
3. recede
4. vacuum
5. vacation
6. vacate
7. intercede
8. proceed
9. concession
10. secede

Page 83

Root It Out

1. evacuate
2. proceed
3. concession
4. vacant
5. intercede
6. vacate
7. vacation
8. secede
9. vacuum
10. recede

Page 84

Combo Mambo

CED, CEED, CESS

1. ceded: yielded or given by treaty
2. antecedent: something that happened or went before something else
3. precedent: following in time, order, or place
4. accessibility: capable of being reached

VAC

1. evacuation: the act of evacuating
2. vacantly: blankly, emptily
3. medevac: an emergency evacuation of the sick or wounded
4. vacuity: an empty space

Read & Replace

Here are some more roots to add to your collection. The root *vac* at the beginning of the word *vacant* means *empty*. The root *ced* at the end of the word *recede* means *go*. (You'll find the same root spelled differently in *proceed* and *concession*.) Read the story. FILL IN the blanks with keywords.

concession	evacuate	intercede	proceed	recede
secede	vacant	vacate	vacation	vacuum

Special Alert:

We need everyone to 1 ______________ the city zoo immediately. We believed that the old snake house was 2 ______________, but we were incorrect. This morning, we sent the janitor in to clean up after the flood waters began to 3 ______________. Judging from the way the janitor dropped his 4 ______________ cleaner and ran away, we were wrong. The zookeeper is out of town on 5 ______________, and we are afraid the snakes will soon 6 ______________ the building and make their way out of the zoo. We are looking for someone to 7 ______________ in this matter. If you are a skilled snake handler, you should 8 ______________ to the zoo immediately. We are willing to make any 9 ______________ to resolve this matter, and we are offering a large reward to anyone who can help us. We do need to be sensitive to the snakes' needs, as the Zoological Society has threatened to 10 ______________ from our Chamber of Commerce if any snakes are harmed.

Check It!

Page 85

Criss Cross

ACROSS
1. proceed
3. concession
6. vacate
7. evacuate
9. vacation
10. secede

DOWN
2. recede
4. intercede
5. vacant
8. vacuum

Page 86

Blank Out!

1. recede
2. vacant
3. evacuate
4. vacuum
5. vacation
6. concession
7. intercede
8. vacate
9. secede
10. proceed

Page 87

It's Puzzling!

1. incessant
2. evacuee
3. accessible
4. evacuator

Page 88

Blank Out!

1. intercede
2. vacuum
3. evacuate
4. concession
5. proceed
6. secede
7. vacate
8. vacant
9. recede
10. vacation

Root It Out

LOOK AT each definition. FILL IN the missing root letters.

HINT: The **bold** words give you a clue about the root. Some roots have alternate spellings.

Root meanings: ced, ceed, cess = go, yield vac = empty, free from

1. If you e____________uate an area during a hurricane, you **empty** it and remove people from danger.
2. The parade will pro____________ when the band **goes** forward and heads down the street.
3. If you make a con____________sion and go to bed early so you can go to the movies on Saturday, you **yield** to your parents' request.
4. If the parking lot is **empty** of cars, it is ____________ant.
5. If two of your friends are having a fight, you might inter____________ and **go** to talk to one of them about it.
6. When you ____________ate your room, you go away from it and leave it **empty**.
7. If you are **free from** school for a week in the winter, you're on ____________ation.
8. If our community decides to se____________ from the town, we will have to **go** and separately form our own township.
9. Outer space is a ____________uum because it is **empty** of all matter.
10. When flood waters re____________, they **go** back to their original level.

Combo Mambo

FILL IN a root in each word. WRITE the word in the column with that root. LOOK UP the definition. Can you see how it's related to its root?

Root meanings: ced, ceed, cess = go, yield vac = empty, free from

_______________ed

e_______________uation

ante_______________ent

_______________antly

mede_______________

pre_______________ent

_______________uity

ac_______________ibility

CED/CEED/CESS *go, yield*	VAC *empty, free from*
1. _______________	1. _______________
2. _______________	2. _______________
3. _______________	3. _______________
4. _______________	4. _______________

Criss Cross

FILL IN the grid by answering the clues with keywords.

ACROSS

1. To continue to do something
3. A privilege given to someone
6. To leave
7. To empty and take to a safe place
9. A period of time when school is closed
10. To separate from an organization

DOWN

2. To grow smaller
4. To come between two groups to settle a disagreement
5. Not occupied
8. Empty space

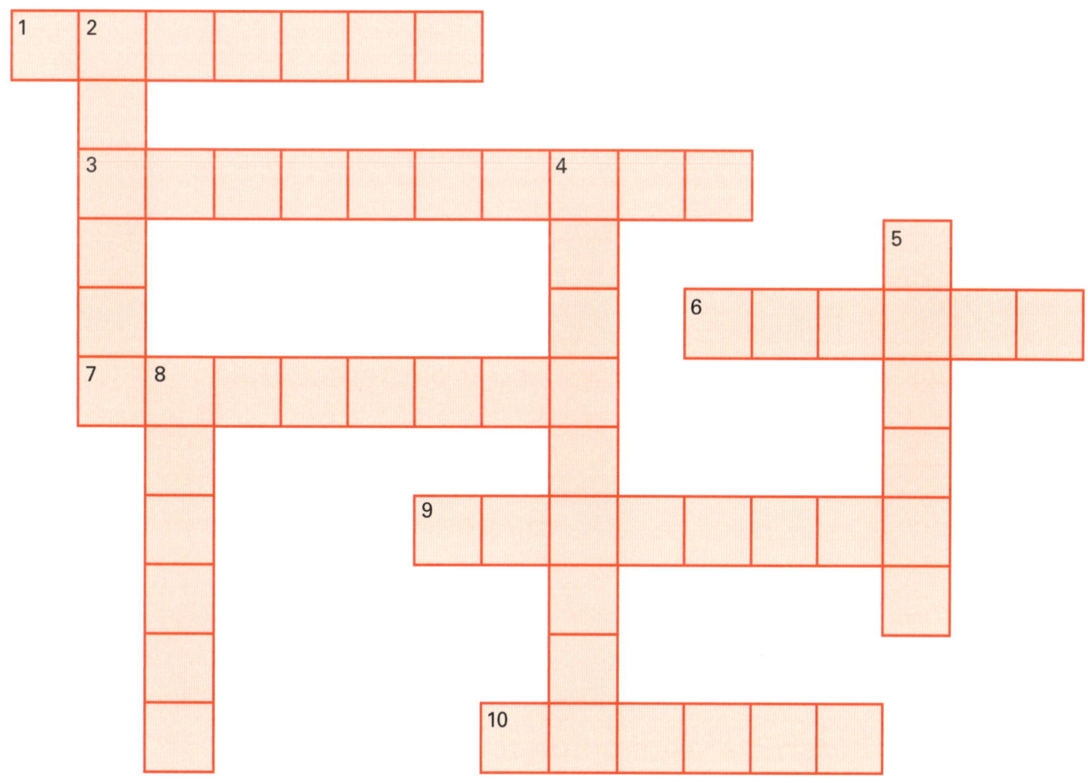

Blank Out!

FILL IN the blanks with keywords.

concession	evacuate	intercede	proceed	recede
secede	vacant	vacate	vacation	vacuum

1. Zander likes to wait until the crowds ________________ before he leaves the stadium after a game.
2. Lana and her friends like to play stickball in the ________________ lot after school.
3. Every year Roger and his family practices how to ________________ their home during a fire.
4. When you suck chocolate milk through a straw, you create a ________________ in your mouth.
5. Christopher's family is going to the shore during summer ________________.
6. The free after-school karate classes are a ________________ for students who maintain a B average.
7. Patrick and his brother wouldn't stop arguing, so their parents had to ________________.
8. The swim team has to ________________ the pool by 10 p.m. on Friday.
9. Our band decided to ________________ from the competition and hold our own Battle of the Bands.
10. Kyle wasn't happy that his parents were going to ________________ with their plan to move to a new state.

It's Puzzling!

MATCH a prefix, root, and suffix together to form a new word. Then WRITE the words in the blanks.

HINT: You can use the same prefix, root, or suffix more than once. If you get stumped, use a dictionary.

Prefixes	Roots	Suffixes
in-	vac	-uee
e-	cess	-ant
ac-		-uator
		-ible

____

____

____

____

Blank Out!

FILL IN the blanks with keywords.

concession	evacuate	intercede	proceed	recede
secede	vacant	vacate	vacation	vacuum

1. If you want your sisters to stop fighting, you should ________________.
2. If there's absolutely nothing in your head at the moment, you might say it is a ________________.
3. You might want to ________________ the room if your little brother's tarantula escapes.
4. If you agree to wash the dishes so you can use the computer later, you are making a ________________.
5. If you're not ready to ________________ up the mountain, you need to take a break before you start climbing.
6. If your group decides to split away from another group, you are going to ________________.
7. If your dad tells you to ________________ the room so he can mop the floors, he means that you should leave.
8. When your next-door neighbors move out, their home will be ________________ until someone else moves in.
9. You can watch the ocean waves ________________ at low tide on the nights after a full moon.
10. If the weather is good, you can go to the pool every day on your ________________.

Keywords

chron•ic—KRAHN-ihk *adjective* 1. lasting a long time 2. always present or encountered

chron•i•cle—KRAHN-ih-kuhl *noun* an account or record of a series of events

chron•o•log•i•cal—krahn-uh-LAHJ-ih-kuhl *adjective* arranged in time order

chro•nol•o•gy—kruh-NAWL-uh-jee *noun* 1. the order in which events occur 2. a list or table of the times and the order in which a series of events occurred

cre•den•tials—krih-DEHN-shuhlz *noun* 1. achievements, training, and background that make a person qualified to do something 2. a letter or certificate that proves someone's position or qualifications

cred•i•bil•i•ty—krehd-uh-BIHL-uh-tee *noun* 1. the ability to inspire belief or trust 2. willingness to accept something as true

cred•it—KREHD-iht *noun* 1. praise or recognition for something achieved 2. a source of honor 3. a person's good reputation or influence

cred•u•lous—KREHJ-uh-luhs *adjective* 1. too ready to believe that something is true 2. resulting from a tendency to believe things too easily

in•cred•i•ble—ihn-KREHD-uh-buhl *adjective* 1. impossible or difficult to believe 2. amazing, unusually good or enjoyable

syn•chro•nize—SIHNG-kruh-niz *verb* 1. to happen at the same time 2. to make something work at the same time or rate as something else

Check It!

Page 90

Read & Replace

1. chronic
2. synchronize
3. credentials
4. chronological
5. chronology
6. chronicle
7. credit
8. incredible
9. credulous
10. credibility

Page 91

Root It Out

1. chronic
2. credentials
3. chronicle
4. incredible
5. chronological
6. credit
7. credulous
8. synchronize
9. credibility
10. chronology

Page 92

Combo Mambo

CHRON
1. chronograph: an instrument for measuring time intervals
2. anachronism: something from another time wrongly placed in a historical setting
3. synchronicity: the quality of happening at the same time

CRED
1. credence: acceptance that something is true or real
2. creditor: a person owed money by another
3. discredit: to make someone appear untrustworthy or wrong
4. credible: having reasonable grounds for being believed
5. accredit: to give official authorization or approval

Read & Replace

Your collection of roots can grow even more! The root *chron* at the beginning of the word *chronic* means *time*. The root *cred* in the middle of the word *incredible* means *belief*. READ the advertisement entry below. FILL IN the blanks with keywords.

chronic	chronicle	chronological	chronology	credentials
credibility	credit	credulous	incredible	synchronize

Late Again? Timekeepers Unlimited Is Here to Help!

Do you suffer from 1 ______________ lateness? Are you unable to 2 ______________ the clocks in your home? Then it's time for you to go to Timekeepers Unlimited. The founders of our organization have the 3 ______________ needed to officially assist you. We begin each meeting with a 4 ______________ account of the previous session. We give our members a chart so they can keep a minute-by-minute 5 ______________ of their day. Next week, our leader will publish a 6 ______________ of our society's history. Our members are a 7 ______________ to society. They show up for every event on time. Their promptness is truly 8 ______________. This is not a gimmick. We are not trying to squeeze money out of 9 ______________ people. You can call the Excellent Business Bureau and ask about our 10 ______________. We'll set your clocks straight once and for all!

Check It!

Page 93

Criss Cross

ACROSS
4. credentials
6. chronological
8. chronic
9. credulous

DOWN
1. credit
2 synchronize
3. chronology
5. credibility
6. chronicle
7. incredible

Page 94

Blank Out!

1. chronological
2. synchronize
3. credibility
4. incredible
5. credentials
6. credulous
7. credit
8. chronology
9. chronicle
10. chronic

Page 95

It's Puzzling!

1. accredit
2. anachronism
3. miscreant
4. incredulous

Page 96

Blank Out!

1. credit
2. synchronize
3. incredible
4. chronology
5. chronic
6. chronological
7. credulous
8. chronicle
9. credentials
10. credibility

Root It Out

READ each definition. FILL IN the missing root letters.

HINT: The **bold** words give you a clue about the root. Some roots have alternate spellings.

Root meanings: *chron = time* *cred = belief*

chronic	chronicle	chronological	chronology	credentials
credibility	credit	credulous	incredible	synchronize

1. If you have a problem that lasts a long **time**, it is ________________ic.
2. A doctor's ________________entials help people **believe** that she is capable of doing her job.
3. An account that is written about events that happened over **time** is a ________________icle.
4. If you find it hard to **believe** something, it is in________________ible.
5. If you put your e-mails in **time** order, they are ________________ological.
6. If people give you ________________it, they **believe** that you are worthy of praise.
7. If your best friend easily **believes** that everything you say is true, he is ________________ulous.
8. If you and another drummer hit your drums at the same **time**, you syn________________ize your beats.
9. If people **believe** and trust in you, you have ________________ibility.
10. When you make a list of the **times** and order in which events happened, it is a ________________ology.

Combo Mambo

FILL IN a root in each word. WRITE the word in the column with that root.

LOOK UP the definition. Can you see how it's related to its root?

Root meanings: *chron = time* *cred = believe*

_______________ence

_______________ograph

_______________itor

dis_______________it

ana_______________ism

_______________ible

ac_______________it

syn_______________icity

CHRON	CRED
time	*believe*
1. _______________	1. _______________
2. _______________	2. _______________
3. _______________	3. _______________
4. _______________	4. _______________

Criss Cross

FILL IN the grid by answering the clues with keywords.

ACROSS

2. Training that makes a person qualified to do something
7. In time order
8. Always present
9. Too ready to believe that something is true

DOWN

1. Recognition for something achieved
2. To make happen at the same time
3. The order in which events occur
5. The willingness to accept something as true
6. A record of events
7. Amazing

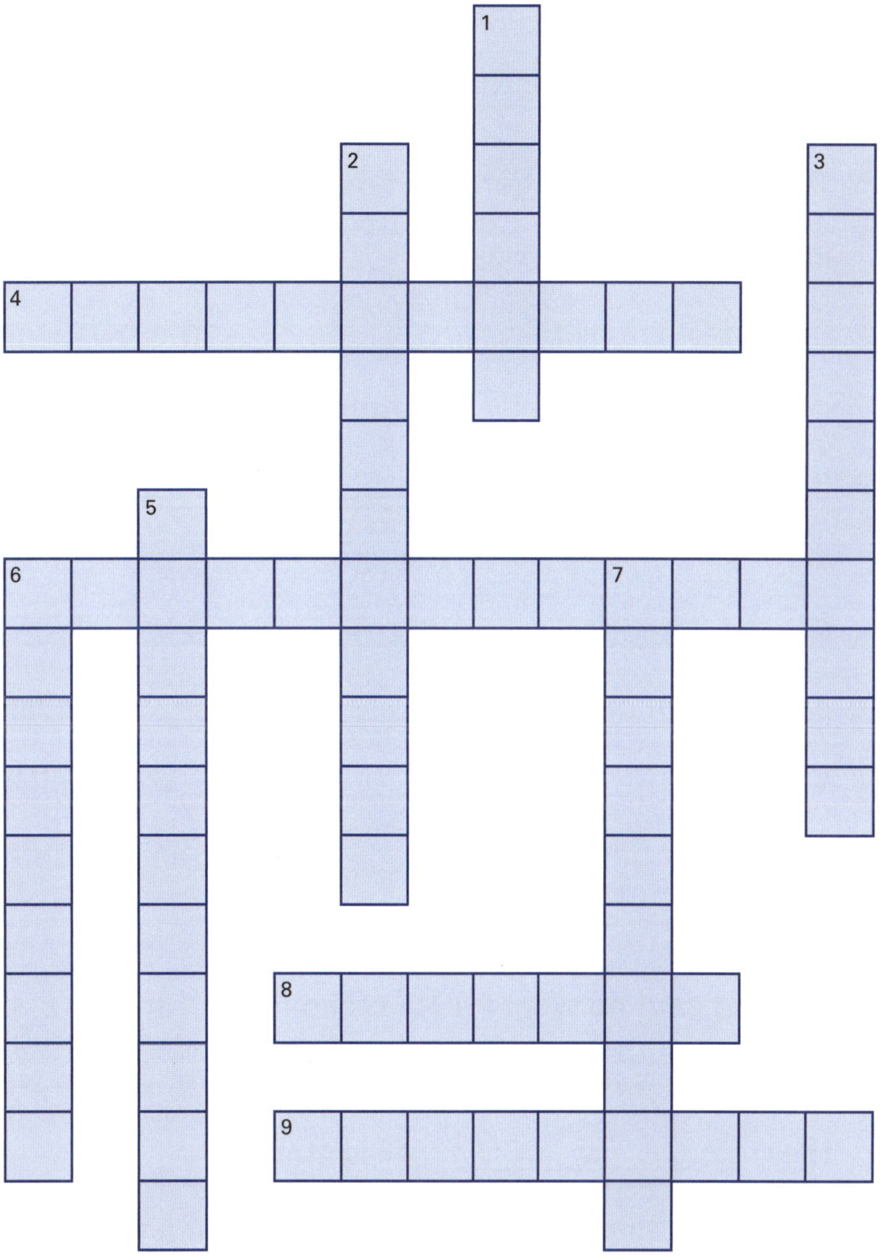

Blank Out!

FILL IN the blanks with keywords.

chronic	chronicle	chronological	chronology	credibility
credit	credentials	credulous	incredible	synchronize

1. Tasha wrote down her race times in ________________ order to see if she had improved with practice.
2. Ed and Olivia will ________________ their watches to be sure they start the competition at exactly the same time.
3. It's hard to trust in Tammy's ________________ after she was caught making up stories for the school newspaper.
4. Garrett thought his new electric guitar was an ________________ present.
5. Jack's mom used her ________________ to get us backstage at the concert.
6. Violet is so ________________ that you could tell her anything and she'd believe it.
7. The mayor gave ________________ to the volunteer firefighters for saving the town hall.
8. Richard said he went for ice cream after the movie, but I saw him walk into the theater with a cone. There's something wrong with the ________________ of his story.
9. Max is reading a ________________ of a pioneer's journey across the country.
10. Flora stopped skating because of her ________________ back pain.

It's Puzzling!

MATCH a prefix, root, and suffix together to form a new word. Then WRITE the words in the blanks.

HINT: You can use the same prefix, root, or suffix more than once. If you get stumped, use a dictionary.

Prefixes	Roots	Suffixes
ac-	cred	-ulous
ana-	chron	-it
mis-	cre	-ant
in-		-ism

____

____

____

____

Blank Out!

FILL IN the blanks with keywords.

chronic	chronicle	chronological	chronology	credibility
credit	credentials	credulous	incredible	synchronize

1. If someone tells you that you did a good job, they are giving you ____________________ for your hard work.
2. It's important for all the members of the dance team to ____________________ their movements.
3. A trip to the moon would be an ____________________ experience.
4. If you write about what happens first, next, and last, you are describing the ____________________ of a story.
5. If you bite your nails every day, you are a ____________________ nail biter.
6. If you put your photos in ____________________ order, you organize them according to the time that they were taken.
7. It is easy to play a trick on someone who is ____________________.
8. A book that tells what happened over a period of time is a ____________________.
9. Your ____________________ tell someone if you have the training you need to do a job.
10. If people know that you always tell the truth, they will trust in your ____________________.

Keywords

an•ti•bi•ot•ic—an-tee-bi-AHT-ihk *noun* a drug or substance that is used to kill bacteria

as•pire—uh-SPIR *verb* 1. to seek to achieve a goal 2. to soar

bi•o•de•grad•a•ble—bi-oh-dih-GRAY-duh-buhl *adjective* capable of being broken down naturally

bi•og•ra•phy—bi-AHG-ruh-fee *noun* 1. an account of a person's life 2. the category of literature that refers to books about people's lives

bi•on•ic—bi-AHN-ihk *adjective* having ordinary human parts or functions replaced by mechanical devices

bi•o•sphere—BI-uh-sfeer *noun* the area of Earth where there are living things

in•spire—ihn-SPIR *verb* 1. to influence or motivate someone to do something 2. to bring about a particular feeling

per•spi•ra•tion—per-spuh-RAY-shuhn *noun* 1. the fluid that comes out of the body through the skin 2. the act of releasing the fluid

res•pi•ra•tion—rehs-puh-RAY-shuhn *noun* the act of breathing air in and out

spir•it—SPEER-iht *noun* 1. a special attitude or state of mind 2. a sense of enthusiasm and loyalty 3. a lively quality

Check It!

Page 98

Read & Replace

1. biography
2. biodegradable
3. biosphere
4. perspiration
5. bionic
6. aspire
7. respiration
8. inspire
9. antibiotic
10. spirit

Page 99

Root It Out

1. respiration
2. biography
3. inspire
4. biosphere
5. biodegradable
6. bionic
7. perspiration
8. aspire
9. spirit
10. antibiotic

Page 100

Combo Mambo

BIO

1. biotechnology: the use of living things in industrial production
2. biopsy: the removal and examination of living tissue
3. biofuel: a fuel made from raw biological materials
4. biodiversity: the range of living things present in an environment

SPIR

1. conspirator: a person who joins in a group that secretly plots against someone
2. transpire: to become known or be revealed
3. aspirant: someone who hopes to attain something
4. uninspired: lacking originality or distinction

Roots, Last Call!

Read & Replace

The root *bio* in the middle of the word *antibiotic* means *life*. The root *spir* at the beginning of the word *spirit* means *breathe*. Read the letter. FILL IN the blanks with keywords.

antibiotic	aspire	biodegradable	biography	bionic
biosphere	inspire	perspiration	respiration	spirit

Dear Albert,

I have finally done it. Soon I will be so famous they will hire an author to write my 1 ____________. You know I have spent years trying to invent a 2 ____________ car that can later be turned into pig food. And you know, after that failed, I began to catalog all the living things in Earth's 3 ____________. Well, you can forget about that project too. It took a lot of hard work (and some smelly 4 ____________), but I may have invented a 5 ____________ brain. You may wonder when I began to 6 ____________ to that goal. It began with my study of human 7 ____________. I wondered how the brain knew to tell the body to breathe. That thought began to 8 ____________ me to dig deeper into the brain. The only problem is that the brain is being attacked by a rare bacteria. My next goal is to create an 9 ____________ to stop the infection. If you have any ideas, please let me know. I have always admired your pioneering 10 ____________.

Your friend,
Wan Tobefamous

Check It!

Page 101

Criss Cross

ACROSS
3. aspire
4. biodegradable
5. respiration
7. biosphere
9. perspiration
10. spirit

DOWN
1. antibiotic
2. biography
6. inspire
8. bionic

Page 102

Blank Out!

1. aspire
2. inspire
3. perspiration
4. respiration
5. antibiotic
6. biography
7. spirit
8. biosphere
9. biodegradable
10. bionic

Page 103

It's Puzzling!

1. aspiration
2. autobiography
3. respiratory
4 biology

Page 104

Blank Out!

1. inspire
2. biodegradable
3. biography
4. aspire
5. antibiotic
6. perspiration
7. respiration
8. bionic
9. biosphere
10. spirit

Root It Out

READ each definition. FILL IN the missing root letters.

HINT: The **bold** words give you a clue about the root. Some roots have alternate spellings.

Root meanings: bio = life spir = breathe

1. The process that makes you **breathe** is re____________ation.
2. A book about the **life** of a person is a ____________graphy.
3. If you **breathe** life into someone's dreams, you in____________e them.
4. The area of the world where you can find **life** is the ____________sphere.
5. Something that can be broken down by **living** things like bacteria is ____________degradable.
6. A mechanical part that acts in place of a **living** organ is ____________nic.
7. When you do something that makes you **breathe** heavily, per____________ation will appear on your skin.
8. When you a____________e to reach a goal, you put every **breath** you take toward reaching it.
9. Your enthusiastic team ____________it is like **breath** of fresh air.
10. An anti____________tic is a drug that kills **living** things such as bacteria.

Combo Mambo

FILL IN a root in each word. WRITE the word in the column with that root.

LOOK UP the definition. Can you see how it's related to its root?

Root meanings: bio = life spir = breathe

con__________ator

__________technology

tran__________e

__________psy

a__________rant

__________fuel

__________diversity

unin__________ed

BIO	SPIR
life	*breathe*
1. __________	1. __________
2. __________	2. __________
3. __________	3. __________
4. __________	4. __________

Criss Cross

FILL IN the grid by answering the clues with keywords.

ACROSS

3. To soar
4. Able to be broken down naturally
5. The act of breathing air in and out
7. The whole area of Earth where there is life
9. The act of releasing fluids through the skin
10. A lively quality

DOWN

1. A drug used to kill bacteria
2. An account of someone's life
6. To bring about a particular feeling
8. Having human parts replaced by machines

Blank Out!

FILL IN the blanks with keywords.

antibiotic	aspire	biodegradable	biography	bionic
biosphere	inspire	perspiration	respiration	spirit

1. I think that Lynn will ____________________ to be an Olympian.
2. Cathy thought about the view from the mountaintop to ____________________ her to climb higher.
3. Nat used a towel to wipe the ____________________ off his face after he finished the bike race.
4. Did you know plants give off oxygen during the ____________________ process?
5. Rita had to take an ____________________ when she had strep throat.
6. Lee is reading a ____________________ of the first woman to fly around the world.
7. The student government is holding a rally to boost school ____________________.
8. All the trees on Earth are part of the ____________________.
9. Wanda likes to use containers made out of ____________________ materials so they won't pollute the Earth.
10. Quincy is learning how to use his new ____________________ hand.

It's Puzzling!

MATCH a prefix, root, and suffix together to form a new word. Then WRITE the words in the blanks.

HINT: You can use the same prefix, root, or suffix more than once, and some words don't have a prefix at all. If you get stumped, use a dictionary.

Prefixes	Roots	Suffixes
a-	bio	-logy
auto-	spir	-graphy
re-		-ation
		-atory

____

____

____

____

Blank Out!

FILL IN the blanks with keywords.

antibiotic	aspire	biodegradable	biography	bionic
biosphere	inspire	perspiration	respiration	spirit

1. A good beat can ____________________ you to get up and dance.
2. The paper you're writing on is ____________________.
3. If someone makes a movie about your life, it's your ____________________.
4. If you ____________________ to be a professional musician, you should practice as much as you can.
5. Your doctor might prescribe an ____________________ for an infection.
6. ____________________ can be a big problem if it leaks through your shirt.
7. Your lungs are the main organs you use for ____________________.
8. Scientists have developed a ____________________ leg that helps a runner keep up with professional athletes.
9. You are a living thing, so you are part of Earth's ____________________.
10. If you're always cheerful and full of enthusiasm, people will admire your ____________________.

Pick the One!

You know your root words, right? So get going and check your skills! LOOK AT each group of words. CIRCLE the real word in each row.

1.	magnitude	magnible	magniature
2.	overcede	intercede	decede
3.	biodulous	biocate	biodegradable
4.	abspire	inspire	prespire
5.	vacate	vacible	vacology
6.	minificent	minimal	minify
7.	chronicle	chronibility	chronable
8.	credulous	credant	credicle

Combo Mambo

WRITE all the words can you make by adding the suffixes to the roots.

HINT: Some suffixes can be used more than once.

Root	Suffix
bio	-ate
magn	-logy
chron	-ic
cred	-it
spir	
vac	

Check It!

Page 105

Pick the One!

1. magnitude
2. intercede
3. biodegradable
4. inspire
5. vacate
6. minimal
7. chronicle
8. credulous

Combo Mambo

1. biology, bionic
2. magnate
3. chronology, chronic
4. credit
5. spirit
6. vacate

Page 106

Match Up

1. d—biology, biosphere, antibiotic
2. f—intercede, proceed, incessant
3. e—chronicle, chronology, synchronize
4. a—credit, discredit, incredible
5. h—magnify, magnate, magnanimous
6. b—minimal, minimum, miniature
7. g—spirit, inspired, aspire
8. c—vacuum, vacate, vacant

Page 107

Pathfinder

1. pro, ceed
2. a, spire
3. ate, magn
4. ant, vac
5. in, spire

Page 108

Sniglets!

1. marathorn
2. octopie
3. telephony
4. overspiration
5. orchistruck
6. dinosore

Match Up

Can you MATCH each root word to its meaning? When you're done, WRITE three words that contain each root.

1. bio	________	a. believe
2. cede	________	b. less, little
3. chron	________	c. empty
4. cred	________	d. life
5. magn	________	e. time
6. min	________	f. go, yield
7. spir	________	g. breathe
8. vac	________	h. great, large

1. ________________ ________________ ________________
2. ________________ ________________ ________________
3. ________________ ________________ ________________
4. ________________ ________________ ________________
5. ________________ ________________ ________________
6. ________________ ________________ ________________
7. ________________ ________________ ________________
8. ________________ ________________ ________________

Pathfinder

The game's the same, only the roots change. Begin at START. When you get to a box with arrows leading you to two different boxes, pick the root that you can add to the prefix or suffix. If you make all the right choices, you'll end up at FINISH.

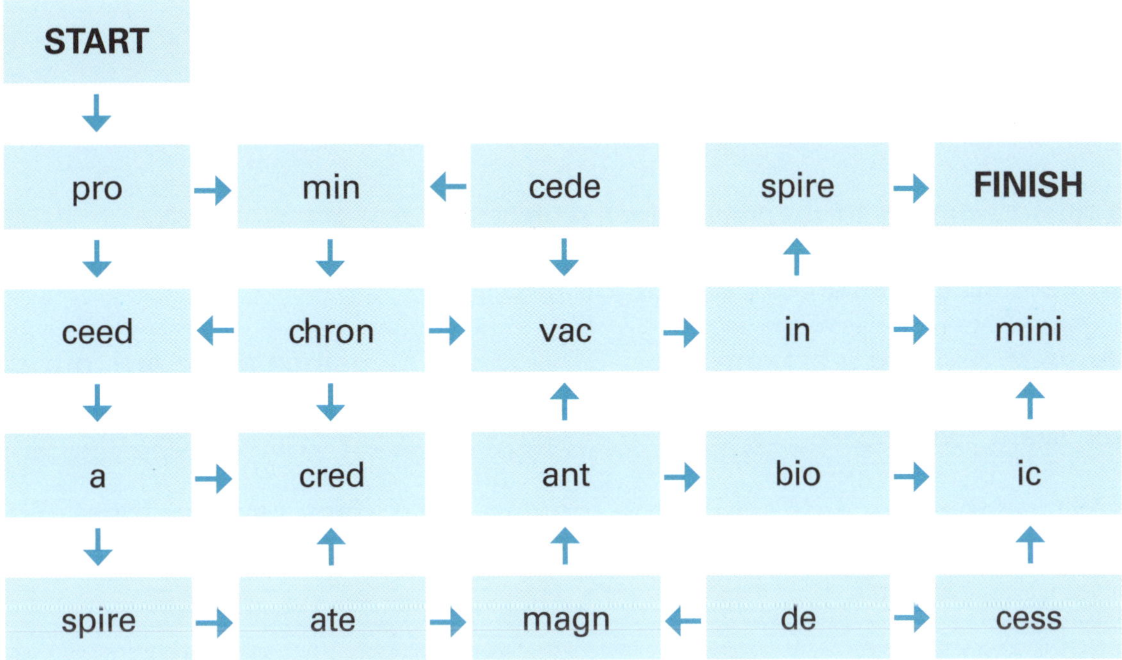

Sniglets!

You're not quite finished with sniglets yet! Here are some sniglets made with root words.

overspiration—the heavy breathing you do when you exercise too much
telephony—someone who lies to you on a phone call
orchistruck—when a French horn falls on you
octopie—a circular food, like pizza, that is cut into eight slices
dinosore—something that's been hurting for a very long time
marathorn—a splinter that stays in your foot for 23 miles

WRITE a sniglet from the list to complete each sentence.

1. Warren needed a tweezer to pull out his ____________________.
2. We'll have to order at least one ____________________, since there are four of us and we each want two slices.
3. Jane told me that she didn't go to the movies, but Tiffany saw her there. She's such a ____________________.
4. We could hear Lenny's ____________________ all the way on the other side of the gym.
5. Marcus's head hurt after he was ____________________ during the concert.
6. Quentin couldn't remember the first time his neck started hurting. It was a real ____________________.

Now it's your turn. Here are some roots you can use to create more sniglets. Use what you know about prefixes, suffixes, and roots to write a definition for each. The sillier the better!

Root

aster = star	hypn = sleep
chrom = color	photo = light
cycl = wheel, circular	sequ = follow
dent = tooth	ultima = last
dynam = power	

____

____

____

____

Vocabulary Words Index

a•board—uh-BAWRD *adverb* 1. on, onto, or into a ship or other vehicle 2. in or into an organization or group

a•bol•ish—uh-BAHL-ihsh *verb* 1. to put an end to something 2. to destroy

ab•sent—ab-SUHNT *adjective* 1. not attending or present 2. not existing 3. not paying attention

ab•sorb—uhb-SAWRB *verb* 1. to take in and make part of the whole 2. to soak up or suck in 3. to hold someone's attention

a•bun•dant—uh-BUHN-duhnt *adjective* present in large amounts or numbers. Synonyms: plentiful, full, ample. Antonyms: empty, lacking.

ad•just—uh-JUHST *verb* 1. to make small changes that make something fit or function better 2. to adapt to a new setting or situation

ad•mire—ad-MIR *verb* 1. to like and respect very much 2. to have a high opinion of

ad•ven•ture—ad-VEHN-cher *noun* 1. an unusual or exciting journey or event 2. a task, trip, or project that involves danger and risk

a•lert[1]—uh-LERT *adjective* 1. watchful and ready to face danger or emergency 2. active and brisk

a•lert[2]—uh-LERT *noun* 1. an alarm or warning of danger 2. a time of careful watching and readiness for danger 3. the period of time when an alert is in effect

am•bas•sa•dor—am-BAS-uh-der *noun* 1. an important official sent to represent a country in a foreign place 2. someone who serves as an official representative of something

an•ces•tor—AN-sehs-ter *noun* someone from the past to whom a person is directly related, usually more distant than a grandparent

an•ti•bi•ot•ic—an-tee-bi-AHT-ihk *noun* a drug or substance that is used to kill bacteria

ap•a•thy—AP-uh-thee *noun* a lack of interest, feeling, or emotion

ape[1]—ayp *noun* a chimpanzee, gorilla, or other tailless mammal in the same family

ape[2]—ayp *verb* to copy or imitate somebody or something

a•shore—uh-SHAWR *adverb* on or to the land from the water

as•pire—uh-SPIR *verb* 1. to seek to achieve a goal 2. to soar

at•ten•dant—uh-TEHN-duhnt *noun* someone whose job it is to serve or help people

a•typ•i•cal—ay-TIHP-ih-kuhl *adjective* not the usual type or kind

be•stow—bih-STOH *verb* to give or present something to someone. Synonyms: give, grant, award. Antonyms: take, get.

bi•o•de•grad•a•ble—bi-oh-dih-GRAY-duh-buhl *adjective* capable of being broken down naturally

bi•og•ra•phy—bi-AHG-ruh-fee *noun* 1. an account of a person's life 2. the category of literature that refers to books about people's lives

bi•ol•o•gist—bi-AHL-uh-jihst *noun* a scientist who studies living things

bi•on•ic—bi-AHN-ihk *adjective* having ordinary human parts or functions replaced by mechanical devices

bi•o•sphere—BI-uh-sfeer *noun* the area of Earth where there are living things

chron•ic—KRAHN-ihk *adjective* 1. lasting a long time 2. always present or encountered

chron•i•cle—KRAHN-ih-kuhl *noun* an account or record of a series of events

chron•o•log•i•cal— krahn-uh-LAHJ-ih-kuhl *adjective* arranged in time order

chro•nol•o•gy—kruh-NAWL-uh-jee *noun* 1. the order in which events occur 2. a list or table of the times and the order in which a series of events occurred

clar•i•fy—KLAR-uh-fi *verb* 1. to make clear or pure 2. to make understandable

com•pre•hend—cahm-prih-HEHND *verb* to understand or grasp the meaning of. Synonyms: understand, get, perceive. Antonyms: misunderstand, mistake.

com•put•er•ize—kuhm-PYOO-tuh-riz *verb* to organize, control, or produce something using a computer

Vocabulary Words Index

con•cen•trate—KAHN-suhn-trayt *verb* 1. to focus attention or thoughts on one thing 2. to draw or bring things closer together 3. to take water out of

con•ces•sion—kuhn-SESH-un *noun* 1. the act of yielding or giving into someone or something 2. a special right or privilege given to someone

con•fi•dant—KAHN-fih-dahnt *noun* a person who is trusted with secrets

con•front—kuhn-FRUHNT *verb* 1. to face someone or something in challenge, to oppose 2. to cause to meet, to bring face to face with something

con•tem•po•rar•y—kuhn-TEHM-puh-rehr-ee *adjective* 1. happening, living, or existing at the same period of time 2. modern or current

con•ver•sa•tion—kahn-ver-SAY-shun *noun* a casual talk with somebody about feelings, ideas, or opinions

cre•den•tials—krih-DEHN-shuhlz *noun* 1. achievements, training, and background that make a person qualified to do something 2. a letter or certificate that proves someone's position or qualifications

cred•i•bil•i•ty—krehd-uh-BIHL-uh-tee *noun* 1. the ability to inspire belief or trust 2. willingness to accept something as true

cred•it—KREHD-iht *noun* 1. praise or recognition for something achieved 2. a source of honor 3. a person's good reputation or influence

cred•u•lous—KREHJ-uh-luhs *adjective* 1. too ready to believe that something is true 2. resulting from a tendency to believe things too easily

de•fend—dih-FEHND *verb* 1. to protect from harm or danger 2. to represent someone in court 3. to offer support for something or someone

de•part—dih-PAHRT *verb* to leave or go away from

de•press—dih-PREHS *verb* 1. to press down or cause to sink 2. to make someone sad 3. to decrease the value of

de•vour—dih-VOWR *verb* to eat up quickly and hungrily. Synonyms: gobble, gorge. Antonyms: fast, nibble.

dis•in•te•grate—dihs-IHN-tih-grayt *verb* 1. to break into small parts, pieces, or elements 2. to destroy the unity or wholeness of something

ea•ger—EE-ger *adjective* enthusiastic and impatiently excited. Synonyms: keen, anxious, impatient. Antonyms: indifferent, reluctant.

e•merge—ih-MERJ *verb* 1. to come out into view, rise, or appear 2. to become known 3. to come to the end of a difficult or bad experience. Synonyms: rise, show, surface. Antonyms: fade, leave.

em•pha•size—EM-fuh-siz *verb* to give importance or draw special attention to something

e•vac•u•ate—ih-VAK-yoo-ayt *verb* 1. to remove from danger 2. to empty

ex•hale—ehks-HAYL *verb* to breathe out

ex•port—ihk-SPAWRT *verb* 1. to carry away or remove 2. to send to another place for sale or exchange

ex•press—ihk-SPREHS *verb* 1. to state in words 2. to show thoughts and feelings through gestures, art, or drama

ex•tra•cur•ric•u•lar—ehk-struh-kuh-RIHK-yuh-ler *adjective* activities that are outside the regular school or work routine

ex•traor•di•nar•y—ihk-STRAWR-dn-ehr-ee *adjective* better or beyond what is typical or regular, extremely good or special

ex•trav•a•gant—ihk-STRAV-uh-guhnt *adjective* 1. beyond what is reasonable or necessary 2. spending or costing an extremely large amount of money

fas•ci•nate—FAS-uh-NAYT *verb* to hold someone's interest or attention completely

fa•tigue—fuh-TEEG *noun* extreme physical or mental tiredness. Synonyms: tiredness, weariness, exhaustion. Antonyms: freshness, energy, vigor.

fra•grant—FRAY-gruhnt *adjective* having a pleasant smell. Synonyms: perfumed, scented, sweet smelling. Antonyms: musty, stinky.

har•dy—HAR-dee *adjective* 1. strong enough to survive difficult conditions 2. bold and daring. Synonyms: rugged, sturdy, strong. Antonyms: delicate, weak.

he•ro•ic—hih-ROH-ihk *adjective* 1. showing great bravery, daring, or courage 2. relating to a hero 3. large in size, power, or effect. Synonyms: brave, daring, mighty. Antonyms: cowardly, timid.

im•mi•grant—IHM-ih-gruhnt *noun* someone who has left his country to go live in another country

in•cred•i•ble—ihn-KREHD-uh-buhl *adjective* 1. impossible or difficult to believe 2. amazing, unusually good or enjoyable

in•fe•ri•or—ihn-FEER-ee-er *adjective* 1. less important 2. of lower quality or value. Synonyms: low grade, shabby, lesser. Antonyms: best, superior.

in•i•ti•ate—ih-NIHSH-ee-ayt *verb* 1. to cause or start something to happen 2. to introduce someone to a new activity, skill, or area 3. to make someone a member of a group, organization, or religion through a special ceremony

in•spire—ihn-SPIR *verb* 1. to influence or motivate someone to do something 2. to bring about a particular feeling

in•ter•cede—ihn-ter-SEED *verb* to come between two people or groups in order to settle a disagreement

in•vade—ihn-VAYD *verb* 1. to enter by force with an army 2. to enter in great numbers or spread over. Synonyms: enter, attack, raid. Antonym: withdraw.

le•gal•ize—LEE-guh-liz *verb* to make legal by making or changing a law

lull—luhl *verb* to soothe or calm. Synonyms: soothe, calm, settle. Antonyms: disturb, alarm.

mag•nan•i•mous—mag-NAN-uh-muhs *adjective* showing kindness, generosity, or forgiveness towards someone

mag•nate—mag-NAYT *noun* a person who has earned a lot of wealth and power in a particular industry

mag•nif•i•cent—mag-NIHF-ih-suhnt *adjective* extremely good, beautiful, impressive, or fine

mag•ni•fy—MAG-nuh-fi *verb* 1. to make something appear larger than it is 2. to increase the size, effect, loudness, or intensity of something 3. to make something appear more important than it actually is

mag•ni•tude—MAG-nih-tood *noun* 1. great size, volume, or scale 2. the importance or significance of something

min•i•a•ture—MIHN-ee-uh-cher *adjective* smaller in size or scale than others of its type

min•i•mal—MIHN-uh-muhl *adjective* 1. very small or slight 2. the smallest or least possible

min•i•mize—MIHN-uh-miz *verb* 1. to reduce or keep to the lowest possible amount or degree 2. to intentionally underestimate the seriousness or extent of something

min•i•mum—MIHN-uh-muhm *noun* the lowest or smallest possible amount or degree of something 2. the lowest degree or amount recorded or allowed by law

mi•nor•i•ty—muh-NAWR-ih-tee *noun* less than half of a larger group

min•ute[1]—MIHN-iht *noun* 1. a period of 60 seconds or one sixtieth of an hour 2. a short period of time

mi•nute[2]—mi-NOOT *adjective* 1. very small 2. of little importance 3. marked by close attention to detail

mis•for•tune—mihs-FAWR-chuhn *noun* 1. bad luck 2. an unpleasant or unhappy event or circumstance. Synonyms: misery, trouble, woe. Antonyms: luck, fortune.

mod•i•fy—MAHD-uh-fi *verb* 1. to change slightly 2. to make less severe or extreme

nav•i•gate—NAV-ih-gayt *verb* 1. to find a course to follow and steer a vehicle there 2. to travel to water 3. to make one's way over or through

op•er•a•tor—AHP-uh-ray-ter *noun* a person whose job it is to run or control a machine

o•ver•flow—oh-ver-FLOH *verb* to flood or flow over the brim or edge

o•ver•take—oh-ver-TAYK *verb* 1. to catch up with and pass by 2. to catch by surprise

o•ver•whelm—oh-ver-HWEHLM *verb* 1. to take over by greater strength, force, or numbers 2. to overpower in thought or feeling 3. to give a large or excessive amount of something to someone

pac•i•fist—PAS-uh-fihst *noun* someone who is against fighting and wars

Vocabulary Words Index

pe•des•tri•an—puh-DEHS-tree-uhn *noun* someone who travels by walking

per•sist—per-SIHST *verb* 1. to continue steadily in spite of problems or difficulties 2. to continue to exist. Synonyms: continue, endure, last. Antonyms: discontinue, stop.

per•spi•ra•tion—per-spuh-RAY-shuhn *noun* 1. the fluid that comes out of the body through the skin 2. the act of releasing the fluid

phy•si•cian—fih-ZIHSH-uhn *noun* a doctor, someone who is qualified to practice medicine

pro•ceed—pruh-SEED *verb* 1. to go on or continue to do something 2. to move in a particular direction

pu•ri•fy—PYUR-uh-fi *verb* 1. to remove harmful or unwanted substances to make something pure 2. to grow or become pure or clean

re•cede—rih-SEED *verb* 1. to move away from or go back from a certain point or level 2. to grow less or smaller

res•pi•ra•tion—rehs-puh-RAY-shuhn *noun* the act of breathing air in and out

se•cede—sih-SEED *verb* to separate or withdraw from an organization, including a country

sen•si•tive—SEHN-sih-tihv *adjective* 1. aware of other's needs, problems, and feelings 2. easily hurt or damaged. Synonyms: delicate, tender, touchy. Antonyms: heartless, insensitive.

spec•ta•cle—SPEHK-tuh-kuhl *noun* a strange or interesting sight. Synonyms: scene, show, wonder. Antonyms: normality, ordinariness.

spir•it—SPEER-iht *noun* 1. a special attitude or state of mind 2. a sense of enthusiasm and loyalty 3. a lively quality

sub•ject[1]—SUHB-jihkt *noun* 1. one who is under the rule of another 2. something that is being discussed, studied, or written about 3. an area of study

sub•ject[2]—suhb-JEHKT *verb* 1. to make someone go through an unpleasant experience 2. to bring under control 3. to expose to something

su•per•in•ten•dent—soo-per-ihn-TEHN-duhnt *noun* 1. a person who manages the way work is done by a group or organization 2. a person who is responsible for taking care of a building

su•pe•ri•or—*suh-PEER-ee-er adjective* 1. better, above average 2. greater in quantity or number 3. higher in rank or importance

su•per•sti•tion—soo-per-STIHSH-uhn *noun* a belief in something that is not real or possible

su•per•vise—SOO-per-viz *verb* to watch over and make sure that a task or activity is being done correctly

syn•chro•nize—SIHNG-kruh-niz *verb* 1. to happen at the same time 2. to make something work at the same time or rate as something else

tri•umph—TRI-uhmf *noun* 1. a great win or achievement 2. a feeling of happiness and pride that comes from success. Synonyms: victory, win, success. Antonyms: loss, defeat.

va•cant—VAY-kuhnt *adjective* 1. not being used, lived in, or occupied 2. showing no signs of thought or expression

va•cate—VAY-kayt *verb* to leave, give up, or withdraw

va•ca•tion—vay-KAY-shuhn *noun* 1. a period of time for rest, travel, and recreation 2. a scheduled period when schools and businesses are closed

vac•u•um—VA-kyoo-uhm *noun* 1. a space that is empty of all matter 2. a device or machine that creates or uses a vacuum

vault[1]—vawlt *noun* 1. an arched roof or ceiling 2. a secure room or compartment for keeping valuables 3. a burial chamber

vault[2]—vawlt *verb* to jump quickly or leap over

vig•or•ous—VIHG-er-uhs *adjective* 1. very strong or active, physically or mentally 2. using or displaying great energy or force. Synonyms: active, forceful, energetic. Antonyms: weak, powerless.

with•er—WIH*TH*-er *verb* 1. to dry up or shrivel 2. to fade or become weak. Synonyms: droop, fade, shrink. Antonyms: bloom, grow.

5th-Grade Reading Comprehension Success

Prepare Yourself 1

Before you dive into a book, take a look at the TABLE OF CONTENTS. What's that? It's a list of the chapters in a book. It may give you a hint about what's inside

Sneak Peak!

Say you're going to read this book:

Electricity: Past, Present, and Future

First, READ the table of contents.

Now, FILL IN the blanks using information from the table of contents.

1. How many chapters does this book have? Five
2. Which chapter might tell you if Ben Franklin invented electricity? I think it is Chapter two
3. Which page does chapter four start on? 27
4. What might be the future of electricity? Solar Power
5. Which two chapters might talk about home lighting?

See how much you can learn from the table of contents?

Check It!

Page 115

Sneak Peak!

1. 5
2. chapter 2
3. 27
4. solar power
5. chapters 1, 4, and possibly 5

Pages 116-117

Sneak Peak!

1. 45
2. knock-knock jokes, animal jokes, holiday jokes, and school jokes, jokes through history
3. pages 10–14
4. pun
5. chapter 7
6. page 45
7. **Suggestion:** You might learn to pause before giving the punch line of a joke.

Pages 118-119

Sneak Peak!

1. chapter 4
2. 8 pages
3. chapter 2
4. chapter 3
5. pages 56–59
6. chapter 5
7. **Suggestion:** Saving the habitat of big cats, or helping stray cats
8. **Suggestion:** A list of books and Web sites about cats

Check It!

Pages 120-121

Sneak Peak!

1. plants, mammals, fish, coral reefs
2. at the bottom of the sea (or chapter 9)
3. chapter 1
4. chapters 10, 11, 13, 14, 16

Suggestions:

5. What creatures can live at the bottom of the sea?
6. How deep into the ocean can humans travel?
7. What is the effect of global warming on the Arctic Ocean?
8. How many oceans are there in the world?

Page 122

Sneak Peak!

Suggestions:

1. When was NASCAR started?
2. How is a stock car different from an Indy 500 car?
3. What happens during a stock car race?

Sneak Peak!

Say you're going to read this book:

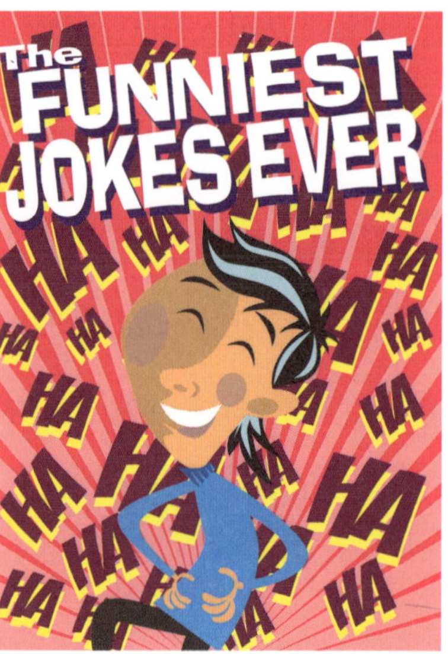

First, READ the table of contents.

Now, FILL IN the blanks using information from the table of contents.

1. At least how many pages does this book have? Eight
2. What kinds of jokes does it cover? all of them
3. Which pages might have a joke about a duck? two
4. What's another word for "a play on words"? puns
5. Which chapter might talk about the oldest joke ever told? Seven
6. Which page has a list of all the jokes in the book? 45
7. What's one thing you might learn in chapter eight?

Sneak Peak!

Say you're going to read this book:

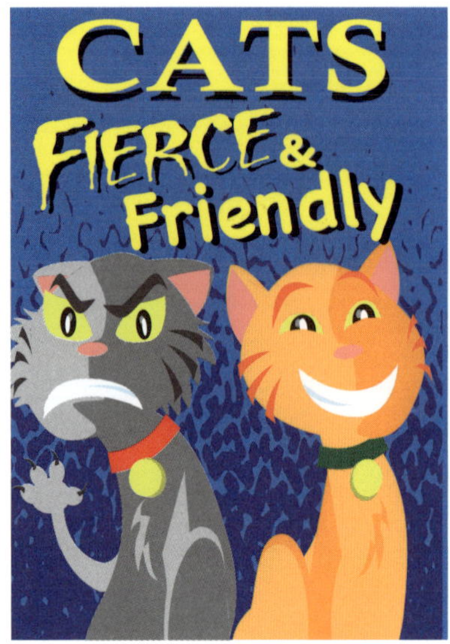

First, READ the table of contents.

Now, FILL IN the blanks using information from the table of contents.

1. Which chapter might describe how cats catch mice? Four
2. How long is chapter seven? 8 pages
3. Which chapter might tell you how many bones a tiger has? ______
4. Which chapter might tell you where leopards live? ______
5. Which pages might tell you about how to treat fleas on your cat? ______
6. Which chapter might cover cats' grooming habits? ______
7. What do you think chapter ten is about? ______

______

8. What do you think you'll find on page 65? ______

______

Sneak Peak!

Say you're going to read this book:

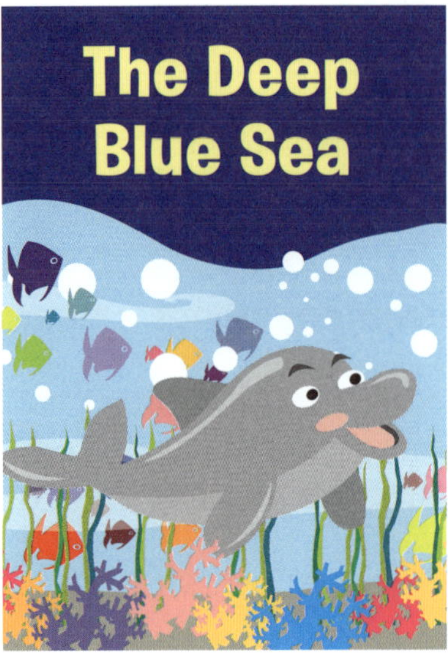

First, READ the table of contents.

Now, FILL IN the blanks using information from the table of contents.

1. What kinds of ocean life does this book cover? ____________________

____

2. Where is "the midnight zone" of the ocean? ____________________

____

3. Which chapter might list the names of the Earth's oceans? ____________________

4. Which chapters might deal with the effect of humans on the oceans?

____

Don't forget, the table of contents is just a clue to all the information in the book. WRITE four more questions that this book might answer that the table of contents can't.

5. ____________________

6. ____________________

7. ____________________

8. ____________________

Sneak Peak!

Say you're going to read this book:

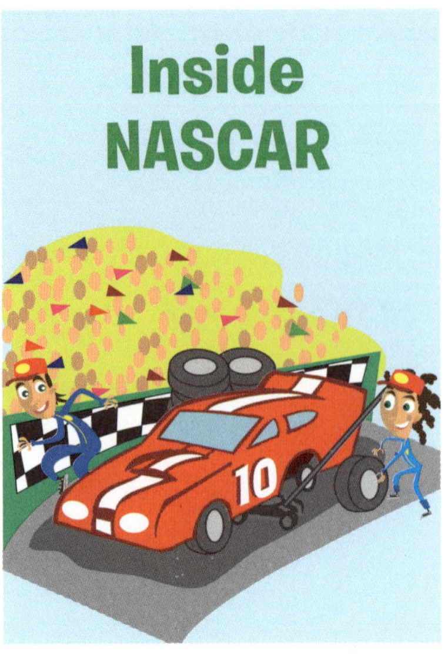

First, READ the table of contents.

WRITE three questions that this book might answer that the table of contents can't.

1. ______________________________

2. ______________________________

3. ______________________________

Check It!

Cut out the Check It! section on page 115, and see if you got the answers right.

2

The table of contents tells you what information is inside a book. But what about the information inside your head? The next step is to think about what you already know about a topic.

First, FILL IN the What Do I Already Know? section. After that, you'll be ready to read!

Topic: Burping

What Do I Already Know?

______

______

______

What Did I Learn?

______

______

______

Now, READ this article.

Excuse Me!

The air that we suck into our lungs contains important gases we couldn't live without. But sometimes we swallow those gases. Then our stomachs have to blast it out. The quickest way is through the mouth—Burrrrrpp! The *other* way can take 30 to 40 minutes. You may pass gas 15 times a day, passing about a quart of gas! Too bad you can't use it to fuel a car, huh?

Time to go back and FILL IN the What Did I Learn? section. CROSS OUT any facts in the first section you got wrong. See how this works?

Check It!

Page 123

Suggestions:

Know:

1. Burping is caused by gas.
2. Some people can burp on purpose.
3. Drinking soda makes you burp.

Learned:

1. Air is filled with gas.
2. Burps move very fast.
3. Every day you pass about a quart of gas.

Pages 124-125

Before & After Questions

Suggestions:

Know:

1. Mount Rushmore is a giant carving of famous heads.
2. It's a big tourist attraction.
3. ~~One of the heads is Ben Franklin.~~

Learned:

1. The monument was built to be a tourist attraction.
2. Susan B. Anthony was proposed as an addition.
3. The monument has only been washed once.

Pages 126-127

Before & After Questions

Suggestions:

Know:

1. Monkeys live in jungles.
2. Monkeys eat bananas.
3. ~~Monkeys and apes are the same thing~~

Learned:

1. Monkeys are not apes.
2. Monkeys also eat insects.
3. NASA sent a monkey into outer space.

Check It!

Pages 128-130

Before & After Questions

Suggestions:

Know:

1. China has the most people.
2. Chinese people celebrate their New Year at a different time than in Western culture.
3. ~~China is smaller than the United states.~~

Learned:

1. China is the most populous country and the third largest in size.
2. Paper, gunpowder, the compass, and printing were invented in China.
3. There are more Chinese restaurants in the United States than there are McDonald's restaurants.

Before & After Questions

FILL IN the What Do I Already Know? section.

Topic: Mount Rushmore

What Do I Already Know?

Every year, two million people vist the Mount Rushmore. it took fourteen year's

What Did I Learn?

It is 60 Foot and 118 meters

Now, READ the article.

Heads of State

Every year, two million people visit Mount Rushmore in South Dakota. And that's a good thing because, from the very beginning, the giant sculpture was meant to be a tourist attraction. A historian named Doane Robinson had the idea in 1923 as a way to bring people to the beautiful Black Hills region of South Dakota.

It took fourteen years for sculptor Gutzon Borglum and 400 workers to sculpt the enormous 60-foot (18-meter) carvings of George Washington, Thomas Jefferson, Theodore Roosevelt, and Abraham Lincoln.

But no ladies were allowed. In 1937, Congress considered adding the head of Susan B. Anthony to the mountain, but the plan fell through. Also, the original plan was for the carvings to include the upper bodies of the presidents, but the money ran out before they could finish.

To take care of the monument, mountain climbers crawl all over the faces every year to find and seal cracks. The presidents have only washed their faces once—in 2005, using a high-pressure hot-water hose!

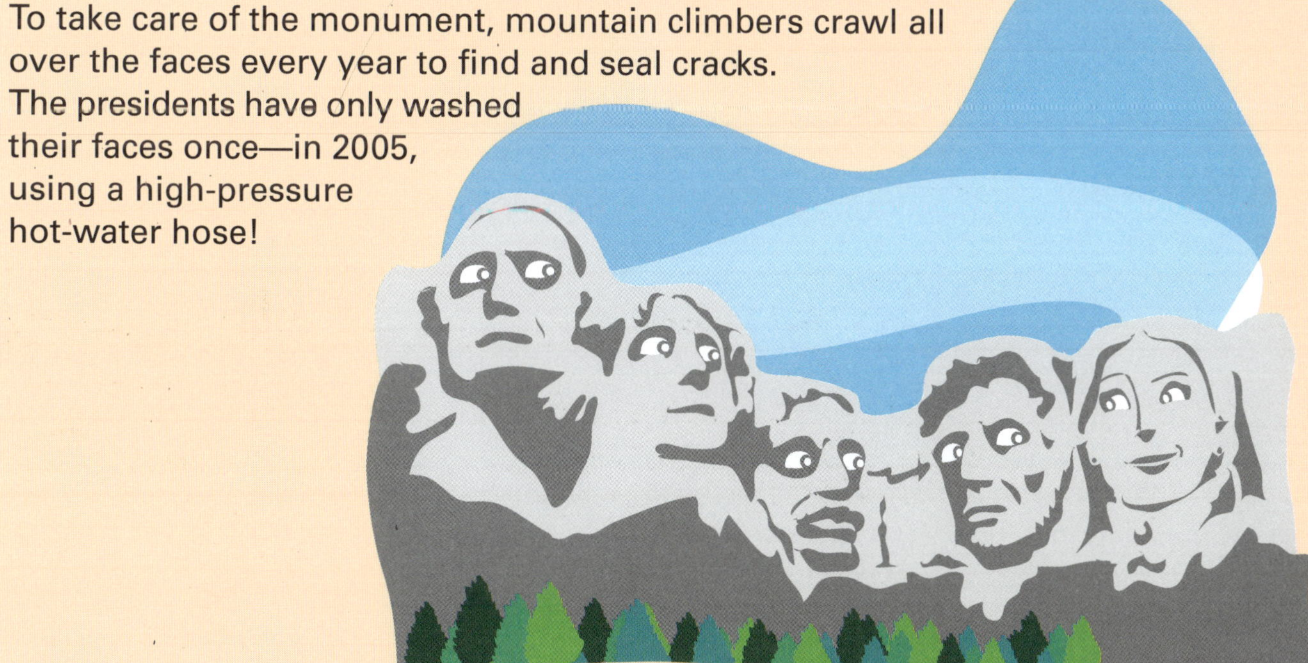

Did you learn anything? Go back and FILL IN the What Did I Learn? section.

Before & After Questions

FILL IN the What Do I Already Know? section.

Topic: Monkeys

What Do I Already Know?

What Did I Learn?

Now, READ the article.

Monkey Business

There are so many kinds of monkeys! More than 200 kinds, to be exact. The smallest monkey is the Pygmy Marmoset, which is only five to six inches long. On the other hand, a big male Mandrill can be three feet tall and weigh 77 pounds. Some monkeys live in the trees, while others live in the dry grasslands called *savanna*.

All monkeys belong to the primate family, but not all primates are monkeys. Lemurs, apes, and humans are also primates. And guess what? Chimpanzees and gorillas aren't monkeys—they're apes. Although most people use the words *ape* and *monkey* to mean the same thing, zoologists know the difference.

Monkeys don't just eat bananas. They eat leaves, flowers, eggs, seeds, nuts, insects, and even crabs!

Some monkeys work hard for their munchies. Scientists often use monkeys in laboratory experiments. Other monkeys are trained to help people who are paralyzed and need an extra hand. (Some monkeys can even grab things with their tails!) NASA has even sent a monkey into outer space.

That's some serious monkey business!

Did you learn anything? Go back and FILL IN the What Did I Learn? section. Don't forget to CROSS OUT any facts in the first section you got wrong.

Before & After Questions

FILL IN the What Do I Already Know? section.

Topic: China

What Do I Already Know?

What Did I Learn?

Now, READ the article.

Land of the Dragon (and the Panda)

China is the most populous country in the world, with around 1.26 billion people. Compare that to the population of the United States, which is just over 300 million. Don't worry, the Chinese have plenty of room. Their country is the third largest in terms of size, with an area of about six million square miles. That's almost twice as big as the United States!

Did you know that the Chinese people have been using written language longer than anybody else? China is also the source of four important inventions: paper, gunpowder, the compass, and printing.

The Chinese dragon is the national symbol because it stands for power in ancient folklore and art. This long dragon usually has the head of a horse or a lion, with horns. The dragon's body is like a snake's, and it sometimes has little bat wings. The Chinese dragon always has sharp, terrifying teeth and may breathe fire through its mouth and nose.

You can see Chinese dragons marching down the street during celebrations of the lunar New Year (in late January or February). They also fly through the air as kites and ride on the water during dragon boat races.

TURN the page to keep reading!

What Do You Know?

Now FINISH reading the article.

The most famous real-life Chinese animal is the giant panda. Today wild panda bears mostly live in the mountains of central China. Over time, the panda has become just as much a symbol of China as the traditional dragon. Since pandas are vegetarians (they mostly eat bamboo), they make a much more peaceful symbol than a fire-breathing monster!

Can you believe there are about 40,000 Chinese restaurants in the United States? That's more than McDonald's, Burger Kings, and KFCs combined! But if you think that fortune cookies are traditional Chinese food, think again! Dishes like chow mein and General Tso's chicken are rarely (if ever) eaten in China. However, it is true that most Chinese people eat food with chopsticks, especially when they're eating out of a bowl.

A big country like China has hundreds of stories and fascinating facts. To learn more, try reading a book about it. (Don't forget to check the table of contents first.)

Did you learn anything? Go back and FILL IN the What Did I Learn? section.

Cut out the Check It! section on page 123, and see if you got the answers right.

3

Fiction authors can be sneaky about giving you information. You may have to read between the lines to get the whole story!

READ this story.

On the Road

Rachel and Lauren bounced in their seat as they traveled down the bumpy road. In front of them, the rows were filled with kids of all ages, shouting and joking. At each stop, a few would get out. This was the best time of the week. One more stop, then Rachel and Lauren would be free for two whole days!

Now, FILL IN the blanks by reading between the lines.

1. Where are Lauren and Rachel?

   ____

   How do you know?

   ____

2. What day of the week is it?

   ____

   How do you know?

   ____

See? A good story doesn't need to spell out every detail—it lets the reader fill in the blanks. Let's do some more!

Check It!

Page 131

1. On a school bus.
   They're bouncing over bumps with rows of children who get off at different stops.
2. Friday.
   They'll have two days free.

Page 132

Blank Out!

1. Talking on a cell phone.
   The reception is bad.
2. His mom or step-mom.
   She's married to his dad.
3. Milk.
   He said "a gallon of skim."

Page 133

Blank Out!

1. Animals.
   They gnaw down trees and have flat tails.
2. She is Barney's mate.
   They built their house together and she's not one of the kids.
3. Fish from the stream.
   Gretel and Hilda find fish for their meal.

Pages 134-135

Blank Out!

1. In a girl's bathroom at school.
   The mirror, the sink, the stall, and fifth period starting. Plus, boys aren't allowed in.
2. Crying.
   Her big hot tears are falling into the sink.
3. She overplucked her eyebrows on one side so they're lopsided.
   She could hide the mistake with sunglasses or a little wig over one eye.
4. A boy.
   He's not allowed in the girl's bathroom.
5. To a dance.
   There's a dress and a tux, and they're sharing a limo.
6. Yes.
   She came out of the stall and smiled.

Blank Out!

READ this story.

Overheard on Hammond Street

"Hello?" hollered Calvin. "Are you there? I lost you for a second. ... Okay, that's better. What? ... I'm on Hammond Street, walking to— ... No, I won't be home for dinner. Dad said it was okay. Yes! I asked him yesterday. ... C'mon! You always do that! Dad says yes, then you say no! Aren't you guys married? You'd think you— ... Well, he didn't tell me that. What time is Grandma coming? ... Okay, okay, I'm coming home now. What? ... All right, I'll stop on my way. A gallon of skim, right? ... Got it. Goodbye!"

Now, FILL IN the blanks by reading between the lines.

1. What is Calvin doing as he walks down the street?

   ____

   How do you know?

   ____

2. Who is he talking to?

   ____

   How do you know?

   ____

3. What is he picking up on his way home?

   ____

   How do you know?

   ____

Check It!

Pages 136-137

Blank Out!

1. Pete.
   He answers when Marcus calls him that.
2. Meat.
   He won't eat any of the meat, he thinks eating meat is animal cruelty, and he wishes there were tofu or greens.
3. At the beach.
   Pete has sand in his shoes, he's worried about getting sunburned, and Marcus is in the waves.
4. Swimming in the ocean.
   He's getting wet in the waves.
5. Volleyball.
   They're bumping a ball back and forth over a net.
6. Talk to Christianne Kendall.
   He wants to trade for her comic book.

Page 138

Author! Author!

Ask a friend to read your story to try to read between the lines!

Blank Out!

READ this story.

Busy Builders

Barney would do anything for his family. He and Hilda had built their house together, tearing down the trees, putting them in place, then filling the cracks so that it was warm and snug. The cozy home was just right for their little clan. Marvin, the oldest, was already helping his dad around the dam. He couldn't gnaw down a whole tree yet, but he could help drag the logs and sticks, and pat mud onto them with his flat tail. The youngest, Gretel, helped her mother find fish in the stream. Occasionally they had trouble with their neighbors, a family of humans who didn't like the way Barney had blocked up the stream. So Barney and Hilda would take their family and move to another spot for a while before coming back to build a new house on the stream. It was the perfect place to raise a family!

Now, FILL IN the blanks by reading between the lines.

1. Are Barney and his family humans or animals?

   ____

   How do you know?

   ____

2. How is Hilda related to Barney?

   ____

   How do you know?

   ____

3. What does Barney's family eat?

   ____

   How do you know?

   ____

Blank Out!

READ this story.

Disaster!

Esther looked into the mirror, her big hot tears plopping into the sink one by one. When she heard somebody opening the door, she scurried into the last stall and locked herself in.

"Esther? Are you in here?" It was Esther's best friend Sofia.

"Leave me alone!" moaned Esther.

"C'mon! It's not that bad. Hardly anybody noticed, I swear!"

"Are you kidding? I look like a freak."

"Okay, so you overplucked on one side. It looks kind of uneven, that's all."

"If only Mr. Woodhouse had let me keep my sunglasses on. Then nobody could see."

"Well, you can't stay in here all day. Fifth period is starting."

Then Terry walked in.

"Hey!" yelled Sofia. "You're not allowed in here!"

"Esther!" called Terry. "Is that you in there?"

"Eek!" screamed Esther. "Get out! Get out!"

"I didn't mean to laugh," said Terry. "And I still want to go on Friday."

"No WAY!" sobbed Esther.

"But I've already got my tux. And you've got your dress!"

"And we're sharing a limo!" added Sofia. "You can wear your sunglasses."

"Or a little wig over one eye," laughed Terry.

"That's not funny!" shouted Esther. But she came out of the stall and smiled.

Now, FILL IN the blanks by reading between the lines.

1. Where is Esther? ____________________

   How do you know? ____________________

   ____

2. What is Esther doing in front of the mirror? ____________________

   ____

   How do you know? ____________________

   ____

3. What is Esther upset about? ____________________

   How do you know? ____________________

   ____

4. Is Terry a boy or a girl? ____________________

   How do you know? ____________________

   ____

5. Where are they all going on Friday night? ____________________

   How do you know? ____________________

   ____

6. Do you think Esther will go with Terry? ____________________

   Why do you think that? ____________________

   ____

Blank Out!

READ this story.

Barbecue Blues

I hate this kind of thing. I can't believe I let Marcus talk me into it. It's only been fifteen minutes, and I already have about six pounds of sand in my shoes. Plus, my skin burns very easily.

"Yo, Pete!" calls Marcus. "Come on in! The waves are great."

"No thanks," I grumble.

Of course, the worst thing is the food. Hot dogs, hamburgers, ribs—I can't eat any of that stuff! That's animal cruelty! When I asked if there was any tofu or greens, everyone looked at me funny. At least there's corn on the cob. And I think the potato salad is safe.

This is so boring! I hate to get wet, so I can't hang out with Marcus. Sure, I could bump a stupid ball back and forth over a net with some other kids, but why? It's all so pointless!

Wait a minute! Things just got a whole lot better. There's Christianne Kendall. She's got a comic book I need for my collection. This is my chance to make her an offer she can't refuse!

Now, FILL IN the blanks by reading between the lines.

1. What's the narrator's name? ____________________

   How do you know? ____________________

   ____

2. What kind of food does the narrator NOT eat? ____________________

   How do you know? ____________________

   ____

3. Where does this scene take place? ____________________

   How do you know? ____________________

   ____

4. What is Marcus doing? ____________________

   How do you know? ____________________

   ____

5. What game are some other kids playing? ____________________

   How do you know? ____________________

   ____

6. What do you think the narrator is going to do next?

   ____

   Why do you think that? ____________________

   ____

Author! Author!

Now it's YOUR turn! WRITE one side of a cell phone conversation between a kid and a soccer coach. (Tell us the kid's side of the conversation.) Here's the trick: you can't use the words *cell phone*, *soccer*, or *coach*. Make sure your reader knows what's up!

HINT: Why is the kid calling the coach? What other words can you use that will let your reader know what they're talking about? What kinds of things do people say when they're talking on cell phones?

✓ Check It!

Cut out the Check It! section on page 131, and see if you got the answers right.

A good book makes you ask questions along the way, like "What will happen next?" A good reader keeps reading to find the answers.

Check, Please!

READ each paragraph, then CHECK the right answers.

Royal Flush

They say King Minos of Crete had one about 2,800 years ago. The ancient Romans had them too. Queen Elizabeth I had a really nice one way back in 1596. But it wasn't until the late 1800s that a plumber named Thomas Crapper made it possible for everyone to have what they needed most.

1. What question does this paragraph want you to ask?

- ☐ a. Where is Crete?
- ☐ b. What year did Elizabeth I become queen?
- ☐ c. What is this thing that King Minos and Elizabeth I had?

Janey's Bad Day

When Janey walked into dance class, everybody stared. They stared as she crossed the room to put down her bag. They stared as she stretched her legs at the barre. And they especially stared when she got into her position on the dance floor.

2. What question does this paragraph want you to ask?

- ☐ a. Is Janey a good dancer?
- ☐ b. Why is everyone staring at Janey?
- ☐ c. Is this a jazz or ballet class?

Check It!

Pages 139-140

Check, Please!

1. c
2. b
3. a
4. c

Pages 141-143

Stop & Go Story

1. What did Duke Kahanamoku do to change the world?
   Underline: Duke Kahanamoku came along and changed the world!
2. What did Duke do next?
   Underline: And that was only the beginning of an amazing career!
3. What was Duke's next career move?
   Underline: His next career move was obvious.
4. How did Duke make headlines with his surfboard?
   Underline: but not the way you'd think
5. What was the surfboard's new job?
   Underline: Duke gave the surfboard a whole new job.
6. What kind of recognition did Duke get in 1965?
   Underline: And in 1965, Duke was finally given all the recognition he deserved.

Pages 144-146

Stop & Go Story

1. What's wrong with Snoop's house?
2. Who's Joey?
3. So who made the mess?
4. Who's at the door?
5. Why is Snoop mad at Missy?
6. Who or what is Fuzzball?
7. Who's gone?
8. What did Snoop find?

READ each paragraph, then CHECK the right answers.

Hanging around the Jungle

In the Amazon jungle, there is an animal like no other. This creature spends a lot of time upside down, hanging from a tree branch. Because his diet is mostly leaves, this mammal doesn't have a lot of energy. So when he moves through the trees (which is rarely), he takes it slow. Really slow.

3. What question does this paragraph want you to ask?

- ☐ a. What is this animal?
- ☐ b. How does this animal live?
- ☐ c. Which part of the Amazon are we talking about?

Mysterious Visitor

Mr. Salazar hated working on Saturdays, but he had a lot to do. By lunchtime, he had already typed up three reports. At the sound of the door opening, Mr. Salazar raised his head. When he saw who was there, the blood drained from his face.

"You!" he gasped. "I thought—I thought you were gone."

"Well," said a voice. "I guess I'm back."

4. What question does this paragraph want you to ask?

- ☐ a. Why is Mr. Salazar so busy?
- ☐ b. What does Mr. Salazar do for a living?
- ☐ c. Who is Mr. Salazar's visitor?

Stop & Go Story

READ the article and FILL IN the blanks along the way.

GO

Wave Rider

In the history of Hawaii, surfing is serious stuff. Ancient leaders used the sport as a training exercise to keep themselves in top physical condition. They also used surfing competitions instead of battles to resolve conflict between people. For a long time, this tradition of surfing was known mainly to the people of Hawaii and other Polynesian cultures. Then Duke Kahanamoku came along and changed the world!

STOP

1. WRITE the question this paragraph makes you ask.

What did Duke Kahanamoku do to change the world?

UNDERLINE the part of the paragraph that makes you ask that.

GO

Duke first became famous as a fabulous swimmer. When he was 21 years old, he broke two world swimming records during an amateur swim meet in Honolulu Harbor. But he was so fast, the official record keepers wouldn't believe it! Not surprisingly, Duke easily made the Olympic swimming team in 1912. Throughout his Olympic career, Duke won three gold medals and two silver medals in swimming. And that was only the beginning of an amazing career!

STOP

2. WRITE the question.

____

UNDERLINE the part of the paragraph that makes you ask that.

Stop and Ask

Keep reading!

When Duke was finished winning medals at the Olympics, he toured the world, giving swimming shows for his fans. He also brought along his surfboard. Duke had been surfing ever since he was a little boy. In 1917, he rode a single wave (caused by an earthquake) for more than a mile! Duke amazed the crowds by riding his 16-foot-long board, sometimes with another person riding behind. Since Duke was handsome and strong, people loved to watch him. His next career move was obvious.

3. WRITE the question.

____

UNDERLINE the part of the paragraph that makes you ask that.

GO

Duke headed for Hollywood. From 1925 to 1955, he made more than 30 movies. And, more importantly, he spent a lot of time surfing on the shores of Santa Cruz, California. Duke wasn't the first person to surf in California, but he was the most famous. As a matter of fact, in 1925 Duke made headlines with his surfboard—but not the way you'd think!

4. WRITE the question.

____

UNDERLINE the part of the paragraph that makes you ask that.

One day, Duke and a few other surfers were hanging out on the beach when a boat capsized not far from shore. The surfers hit the waves with their big boards and saved 12 of the passengers. Duke alone saved eight of them! At the same time, Duke gave the surfboard a whole new job.

5. WRITE the question.

____

UNDERLINE the part of the paragraph that makes you ask that.

GO

After Duke's big rescue, lifeguards at beaches started using surfboards to rescue swimmers. Helping others was a big theme in Duke's life. In 1932, Duke became sheriff of Honolulu, Hawaii. Following in the footsteps of his father, who was a police officer, Duke served as sheriff for almost 30 years. His job as sheriff was to greet visitors who came to the city. It was a perfect fit. From the Olympics to Hollywood, Duke Kahanamoku had put Hawaii on the map when it was still a remote island. He was truly the "Ambassador of Aloha." And in 1965, Duke was finally given all the recognition he deserved.

STOP

6. WRITE the question.

____

UNDERLINE the part of the paragraph that makes you ask that.

GO

When he was 75 years old, Duke's name was added to both the Swimming Hall of Fame and the Surfing Hall of Fame. The record keepers who didn't believe in his first world record had apologized long before. As an athlete and an ambassador, Duke Kahanamoku had always been a legend, and now it's official!

Stop & Go Story

READ the story and FILL IN the blanks along the way.

Snoop is on the Case!

Famous kid detective Snoop Rodriguez found a major mystery waiting for him when he got home from school one day. He stopped dead in his tracks when he opened his front door.

"What the—?" He looked around the living room in astonishment. Then he raced through the house. Every room was the same. "I better get to the bottom of this," he said.

1. WRITE the question this paragraph makes you ask.

____

GUESS the answer to your question.

____

Snoop went back to the living room and looked more closely. Everything had been knocked off the low tables onto the floor. His mother's favorite china frog was in pieces. And there were little black marks of mud on the floor, the furniture, even on the low part of the walls.

"Joey!" cried Snoop. "This mess has 'Joey' written all over it."

2. WRITE the question. ____________________________

GUESS the answer. ____________________________

GO

Snoop ran into his backyard. Joey was there, tied to his doghouse as usual. His tail thumped the ground at the sight of Snoop.

"All tied up, huh, boy?" said Snoop, rubbing Joey's ears. He checked the little dog's paws. "No mud," he said. "I guess you're in the clear. Hmm...."

3. WRITE the question. ____________________________

GUESS the answer. ____________________________

GO

Snoop went back inside and cleaned up the living room. He left some of the paw prints because they were important clues. While he was finishing up, the doorbell rang. Snoop opened the door and made a sour face.

"What do *you* want?" he asked.

STOP

4. WRITE the question. ______________________________

GUESS the answer. ______________________________

Missy Peterson didn't wait to be invited in. She swept past Snoop and sat down on the couch.

"I need your help," she said.

"And why should I help you?" asked Snoop. He still stood by the door as if he wanted her to leave.

Missy laughed. "Are you still mad? C'mon Snoopy! It's been three months!"

5. WRITE the question. ______________________________

GUESS the answer. ______________________________

"Yeah," said Snoopy. "Three months since you wrecked my bike and got me grounded."

"It was all for a good cause," said Missy. "We found Fuzzball, right? And I owe you big time."

"Great," said Snoop. "So do me a favor and leave. I'm busy."

"I can't leave," said Missy. "Fuzzball is missing again!"

6. WRITE the question. ______________________________

GUESS the answer. ______________________________

Stop and Ask

Keep reading!

"Fuzzball!" cried Snoop. He raced over to the paw prints. "Yes, it could be, but—wait! There are two sets of prints here."

"What are you talking about?" said Missy.

Just then, the door flew open and Tariq Singleton ran in. "Snoop! You've got to help me! She's gone! I've looked everywhere, but she's gone!"

7. WRITE the question. ______________________

GUESS the answer. ______________________

"Let me guess," said Snoop. Things were getting clearer now. "Miss Kitty has run away, right?"

"Wow," said Tariq. "You really ARE a great detective!"

"I think I know who made the mess in my living room," said Snoop. "But there's one last puzzle I need to solve." He started looking at all the windows very carefully. "A-ha!"

8. WRITE the question. ______________________

GUESS the answer. ______________________

"This window is open!" said Snoop. "I bet Fuzzball ran in here, and Miss Kitty chased him all over the house. But where are they now?"

"Let's search the house!" yelled Tariq.

The three kids ran from room to room. Finally, in the basement, they found what they were looking for. Fuzzball the ferret was curled up on the washing machine, fast asleep. Miss Kitty was on the dryer, snoring.

"I guess they wore themselves out," said Snoop. "Now help me clean up the rest of the house before my mom gets home!"

Books and stories can be packed with information. But don't worry! Nobody expects you to memorize it as you read. It's okay to go back and reread, or to do a quick CROSS CHECK to refresh your memory.

READ this article.

Shake Up Some Ice Cream!

You can't have ice cream without ice, right? Back in the old days before refrigerators and freezers, the only way to get ice was to cut it from frozen ponds or lakes in the winter. So making ice cream was really hard.

Making your own ice cream is pretty easy nowadays, if you have the time and some ice cubes!

Ingredients:
2 tablespoons of sugar
1 cup of half and half
½ teaspoon of vanilla extract
½ cup of kosher or rock salt
One small and one large resealable bag
Your favorite ice cream toppings
Lots of ice cubes!

Mix the half and half, sugar, and vanilla in the smaller resealable bag. Seal it up tight. Put the ice in the bigger bag with the salt. Before you seal it, put the smaller bag inside too. Then seal the big bag and get shaking! Keep the ice moving all around the smaller bag, so that the half and half freezes up. It should take about 5 to 10 minutes.

When the small bag feels like ice cream, take it out, throw in your fave toppings, and eat. Yum!

Now, TURN the page to answer some questions.

Check It!

Pages 147-148

1. From frozen lakes and ponds in the winter
2. 1 cup
3. 2
4. The smaller one holds the ice cream ingredients, and the larger one holds the ice and salt that freezes it.
5. Shake the resealable bags.
6. Add your favorite toppings!

Pages 149-150

Stop & Go Story

1. super-strong metal, super-fast elevators, and super-cool air conditioning
2. both 40 Wall Street and the Chrysler Building
3. because there's not a lot of room to spread out in cities
4. the Empire State Building
5. 1,670 feet tall
6. in Malaysia

Pages 151-152

Stop & Go Story

1. Snoop Rodriguez
2. Book #7
3. Thursday
4. Brooke
5. Cheryl
6. #6 and #8
7. Thursday
8. Cheryl

Pages 153-154

Stop & Go Story

1. about 43 hours
2. 500,000 gallons
3. air leaks
4. flight deck inspection
5. T–9 minutes
6. Kennedy Space Center in Cape Canaveral, Florida
7. Mission Control in Houston, Texas
8. 3 hours

FILL IN the blanks by answering the questions if you can.
DON'T ANSWER if you can't remember (and don't reread yet!).

1. Where did ice come from before we had refrigerators and freezers?

   ____

2. How much half and half do you need to make ice cream?

   ____

3. How many resealable bags do you need?

   ____

4. What do you use the resealable bags for?

   ____

5. What do you have to do to freeze the ice cream?

   ____

6. What's the very last thing you should do before eating?

   ____

How many blanks did you leave empty? ______________________________

Okay, now go back and CROSS CHECK the questions with the article to FILL IN any missing answers.

Stop & Go Story

READ the article and FILL IN the blanks along the way.

Race for the Sky

In big cities, there's not a lot of room to spread out. But there's plenty of space if you build up—in fact, the sky's the limit!

We wouldn't have skyscrapers without technology. Tall buildings need super-strong metal to support the weight of so many stories. They also need super-fast elevators to get people to the top. And they need super-cool air conditioning to keep everyone from boiling over (it gets hot on the 100th floor!). Today's skyscrapers are really superbuildings!

They just keep getting taller. In 1930, the tallest building in the world was at 40 Wall Street in New York City (927 feet tall). But not for long! Later that year, the Chrysler Building became the tallest building (1,046 feet). But not for long! In 1931, the Empire State Building (1,250 feet) was finished.

The Empire State Building ruled the roost for more than 40 years. Then in 1971, the World Trade Center (1,368 feet) became the tallest building in the world. But not for long! Three years later, the Sears Tower in Chicago (1,454 feet) grabbed the title. It lasted until 1998 when it was overtaken by the Petronas Twin Towers in Malaysia (1,483 feet). And in 2004, Taipei 101 in Taiwan (1,670 feet) became the tallest building in the world. But not for long!

Now, TURN the page and FILL IN the blanks.

Cross Check

FILL IN the blanks by answering the questions if you can.
DON'T ANSWER if you can't remember (and don't reread yet!).

1. What three things make skyscrapers possible?

____

2. What was the tallest building in 1930? Hint: This is a trick question.

____

3. Why do we build skyscrapers so high?

____

4. Which skyscraper was the tallest building for the longest time?

____

5. How tall is Taipei 101?

____

6. Where are the Petronas Twin Towers?

____

How many blanks did you leave empty? ______________________________

Okay, now go back and CROSS CHECK the questions with the article to FILL IN any missing answers.

Finally, FINISH the article!

The race to the sky isn't finished yet. The Burj Dubai in the United Arab Emirates is the world's tallest structure at over 2,000 feet tall. And there are other buildings in the works that might go even higher, including a Mile-High Tower in Saudi Arabia!

Stop & Go Story

READ the story and FILL IN the blanks along the way.

The Mystery of the Missing Mystery

"Okay, confess!" hollered Shakeel. "You borrowed #7 without asking!"

"What are you talking about?" asked his twin sister Brooke. "What's #7?"

"Book seven of *Snoop Rodriguez: Kid Detective!* See? It's supposed to be right on my shelf between #6 and #8, but it's not there!"

"Well, I didn't take it, so stop shouting! Where did you see it last?"

Shakeel thought a minute. Since his Snoop Rodriguez books were really popular, he kept track of them carefully, just like a librarian. So he looked at his notes from last week:

Monday: Eli borrowed #2. Indira returned #7.

Tuesday: Cheryl took #6. Robyn returned #8.

Wednesday: Nadine took #1. Ralph took #5.

Thursday: SCOUT HIKE ALL DAY

Friday: Steven took #10. Eli returned #2 and took #3.

Shakeel showed the list to his sister.

"I think it's pretty obvious," Brooke said. "Just look at your shelf, then ask Mom if anyone came by on Thursday while you were away."

Now, TURN the page and FILL IN the blanks.

Cross Check

FILL IN the blanks by answering the questions if you can.
DON'T ANSWER if you can't remember (and don't reread yet!).

1. What's the name of the detective that stars in Shakeel's books?

____

2. Which book is missing? ______________________________

3. What day was Shakeel at the scout hike? ______________________________

4. What is Shakeel's sister's name? ______________________________

5. Who borrowed book #6 on Tuesday? ______________________________

6. What two books does Shakeel say are on his shelf? ______________________________

7. When do you think book #6 was returned? ______________________________

8. So who probably has book #7? ______________________________

How many blanks did you leave empty? ______________________________

Okay, now turn back and CROSS CHECK the questions with the article to FILL IN any missing answers.

Finally, FINISH the article!

Shakeel took Brooke's advice and asked his mom. She told him his friend Cheryl had come by on Thursday while he was on the scout hike. She had returned book #6 and borrowed book #7.

"I'm sorry!" Mom said. "It totally slipped my mind."

Mystery solved!

Stop & Go Story

READ the article and FILL IN the blanks along the way.

We Have Liftoff!

The big countdown clock at NASA's Kennedy Space Center lights up about 43 hours before the space shuttle takes off. When the space shuttle is in orbit, it's managed by Mission Control in Houston, Texas. But Launch Control is at Kennedy Space Center in Cape Canaveral, Florida, where the big countdown clock stands in a field. There's about a million things to do to get ready! Here's a sampling:

From T–43 hours (that's "launch time minus 43 hours") to T–20 minutes, the shuttle team checks the steering system and engines. They also load the fuel cells and inspect the flight deck, where the crew will sit and fly the shuttle.

Everyone has to get off the launch pad at T–6 hours because the external fuel tank is being filled with 500,000 gallons of propellants—very dangerous stuff!

The crew enters the shuttle at T–3 hours and begins the last-minute system checks. The shuttle hatch is closed and checked for air leaks. Everyone else clears out.

T–9 minutes and counting! This is when the shuttle team decides whether the launch is really "a go." If so, the bridge leading to the shuttle is retracted (T–7), the shuttle powers up (T–5), there's a final engine test (T–3), the crew members lock their visors (T–2), the sound mufflers are turned on (T–16 seconds), and the main engine is lit (T–6.6 seconds).

T–0 seconds—the rocket booster ignites. We have liftoff!

FILL IN the blanks by answering the questions if you can.
DON'T ANSWER if you can't remember (and don't reread yet!).

1. At how many hours before liftoff does the countdown clock start?

____

2. How many gallons of propellants does the shuttle fuel tank need?

____

Cross Check

3. When you check the shuttle hatch, what are you looking for?

____

4. Which happens first, flight deck inspection or final engine test?

____

5. When does the team decide whether the launch is a go?

____

6. Where is Launch Control located?

____

7. Who manages the shuttle while it's in orbit?

____

8. How much time does the crew spend in the shuttle before liftoff?

____

How many blanks did you leave empty? _______________

Okay, now go back and CROSS CHECK the questions with the article to FILL IN any missing answers.

Finally, FINISH the article!

GO

About two weeks and 5.7 million miles later, the space shuttle lands again at Kennedy Space Center. If the weather isn't right in Florida, there's a backup landing field for the shuttle at Edwards Air Force Base in California. When it lands there, how does the shuttle get back to Florida for its next mission? It flies piggyback on top of a special airplane! Pretty cool, huh?

You can learn lots of new words as you read. When you stumble on a word you don't know, use the words around it to figure out what it means. Let's see how this works.

READ this paragraph.

Last winter, my brother and I were sledding down Loggers Hill when I crashed into a tree. I got a cut on my arm that was so big it needed seventeen stitches! Even a year later, there's a long, snaky scar on my arm where the cut was. It's really impressive—I show it to all the kids. Most of them think it's really cool, except for the girls, who think it's gross!

So do you know what *scar* means?

1. Is *scar* a noun (object), a verb (action), or an adjective (description)? ______
2. Where is this kid's scar? ______
3. What happened to this kid's arm? ______
4. What is a scar? ______

See, you figured it out. And now you know a new word. Keep going!

Check It!

Page 155

1. noun
2. on his arm
3. He got a big cut on it.
4. It's a mark left behind by a wound.

Page 156

What's the Word?

1. adjective
2. She laughed as if she didn't care.
3. She apologized and helped clean up.
4. She cried because she was sorry she broke the bowl.
5. sorry

Page 157

What's the Word?

1. noun
2. He was on the porch.
3. He was inside the house.
4. He crossed it.
5. doorway or entrance

Page 158

What's the Word?

1. verb
2. down the street
3. on foot
4. He's really proud and vain.
5. to walk as if you're the best thing ever

What's the Word?

Before you read the paragraph, answer this question:

What do you think the word *contrite* means? (It's okay to guess!)

___

Now READ this paragraph and see if you change your mind.

I was babysitting for three-year-old Grace when she broke her mom's favorite china bowl. At first, Grace laughed as if she didn't care at all. Then she saw how upset I was and she became contrite. She said she was sorry and helped me clean up. She even cried a little! Then I helped her write an apology for her mom. Grace is a good kid!

1. Is *contrite* being used as a noun, adjective, or verb?

   ___

2. How did Grace act when she first broke the bowl?

   ___

3. What did Grace do when she was *contrite*?

   ___

4. Why did Grace cry?

   ___

5. Now, what do you think the word *contrite* means?

   ___

Check It!

Page 159

What's the Word?

1. noun
2. a person
3. professional
4. Amateurs don't play for money.
5. someone who does something because they enjoy it, not for the money

Page 160

What's the Word?

1. adjective
2. the change in the lady's manner
3. She treated him nicely.
4. just a second
5. sudden, quick

Pages 161-162

What's the Word?

1. verb
2. move
3. the surface of the ocean
4. the bottom of the ocean
5. down
6. to go down
7. noun
8. the ship
9. metal, broken dishes, jewelry, coins
10. They're considered debris because they came off a wrecked ship.
11. junk that's leftover from a wreck

What's the Word?

What do you think the word *threshold* means? (It's okay to guess!)

____

Now READ this paragraph and see if you change your mind.

The soldier stood on the porch, waiting for word from his commander. Mama loomed on the other side of the open doorway, blocking his way into the house. He looked as nervous as I was. Finally his walkie-talkie beeped, and he got his instructions. "I'll have to search the place, ma'am," he said politely.

At that, Mama stepped back, allowing the soldier to cross the threshold into our home.

1. Is *threshold* being used as a noun, adjective, or verb?

   ____

2. Where was the soldier at the beginning of the story?

   ____

3. Where was the soldier at the end of the story?

   ____

4. What did the soldier do with the *threshold*?

   ____

5. Now, what do you think the word *threshold* means?

   ____

What's the Word?

What do you think the word *swagger* means? (It's okay to guess!)

Now READ this paragraph and see if you change your mind.

I can't stand Eddie Ross! Everything about him makes me mad. Look at that leather jacket! Does he think he's some kind of tough guy? And he always calls me "babe." Grrr! I especially hate the way he swaggers down the street, with his thumbs in the pockets of his jeans, swinging his hips like he owns the entire planet. Ew! He just *winked* at me. I guess he thinks he's hot or something. As if!

1. Is *swagger* being used as a noun, adjective, or verb?

2. Where does Eddie *swagger*?

3. Does Eddie *swagger* in a car or on foot?

4. What kind of guy is Eddie?

5. Now, what do you think the word *swagger* means?

What's the Word?

What do you think the word *amateur* means? (It's okay to guess!)

Now READ this paragraph and see if you change your mind.

When the modern Olympic Games began, professional athletes were not allowed to compete. The Games were supposed to feature amateurs who played for love of the sport, not money. In 1912, one athlete was kicked out of the Games because he had once been paid to play baseball. But in the 1970s, the rules against professionals were dropped. When the United States decided to use highly paid NBA basketball stars instead of amateurs, they called them "The Dream Team." Gold medal? No problem!

1. Is *amateur* being used as a noun, adjective, or verb?

2. Is an *amateur* a person, a place, or a thing?

3. In this paragraph, what is the opposite of *amateur*?

4. How is an *amateur* different from its opposite?

5. Now, what do you think the word *amateur* means?

What's the Word?

What do you think the word *abrupt* means? (It's okay to guess!)

Now READ this paragraph and see if you change your mind.

When Herbie first walked into the bank, the lady behind the desk was kind of rude. She acted like he was wasting her time. After all, what business would a kid like Herbie have at a fancy bank? But when he pulled out the big wad of money he had been saving, the lady had an abrupt change in personality. The second she saw that stack of bills, she got all nicey-nice. She even called Herbie "sir"!

1. Is *abrupt* being used as a noun, adjective, or verb?

2. What does the word *abrupt* describe?

3. What happened when the lady saw Herbie's money?

4. How long did it take for the lady to change her manner toward Herbie?

5. Now, what do you think the word *abrupt* means?

What's the Word?

Let's do two words this time!

What do you think the word *descend* means? (It's okay to guess!)

____

What do you think the word *debris* means? (It's still okay to guess!)

____

Now READ this paragraph and see if you change your mind.

To see the wreckage of the *Titanic*, you need a boat to take you 370 miles off the shore of Newfoundland, Canada. You'll also need a submarine to get you to the bottom of the ocean. That's about two miles down! After you descend from the surface to the bottom, the first thing you will see is the front of the ship, almost whole. The *Titanic* broke into two parts as it sank. On the ocean floor, between the two halves, is a wide area of debris from the ship. From the window of your submarine, you may see pieces of metal, broken dishes, jewelry, even some silver coins. But you can't take anything—the site is a memorial to the 1,517 people who died in the wreck.

1. Is *descend* being used as a noun, adjective, or verb? ____________________
2. When you *descend*, do you move or stay still? ____________________
3. Where do you *descend* from? ____________________
4. Where do you *descend* to? ____________________
5. So what direction do you go when you *descend*? ____________________
6. Now, what do you think the word *descend* means?

   ____

TURN the page to work on *debris*.

FILL IN the blanks to figure out the word.

Tip: Some words aren't pronounced the way you'd think. In *debris* you don't pronounce the "s" at the end (duh-BREE).

7. Is *debris* being used as a noun, adjective, or verb?

____

8. Where did the *debris* come from?

____

9. What objects are considered *debris*?

____

10. Why are those objects considered *debris* now?

____

11. Now, what do you think the word *debris* means?

____

Make an Argument 7

Everyone has a right to his or her opinion. But to make an ARGUMENT, you need to back up your opinion with some facts. Can you tell the difference between an opinion and an argument?

READ each statement. CIRCLE A for *argument*, F for *fact*, and O for *opinion*.

1. Blue is the prettiest color in the whole world. A F O
2. Tiffany is taller than Hamid. A F O
3. Kids should vote because they're affected by laws too. A F O
4. Cable TV should be free because I love it! A F O
5. If a kid is old enough to babysit, he doesn't need a sitter. A F O
6. Going for a swim might cool you off. A F O
7. Of course fairies are real! A F O

WRITE an example of a fact.

___

WRITE an example of an opinion.

___

WRITE an example of an argument.

___

When you read an argument, you should see how many FACTS support the OPINION.

Check It!

Page 163

1. O
2. F
3. A
4. O
5. A
6. F
7. O

Suggestions:
Fact: The earth is round.
Opinion: Reggae music is cooler than rock.
Argument: Flying is safer than driving because there are way more car accidents than plane crashes.

Pages 164-165

Suggestions:
YES! Biggie Burger should open.
Facts:
1. The restaurant serves low-priced food.
2. Teenagers can get jobs there.
3. It will bring tax money to the town.
4. People coming to Biggie Burger might shop nearby.

NO! Biggie Burger should not open.
Facts:
1. Fast food is high in salt, fat, and sugar.
2. It might bring strangers to the area.
3. It might take business away from local restaurants.

Pages 166-167

Suggestions:
Quit soccer:
1. more time for homework
2. try a new activity
3. more time for extra chores
4. could make new friends

Stay on team:
1. really good at soccer
2. might be captain next year
3. on the team for two years
4. loves soccer
5. has lots of soccer buds

Check It!

Pages 168-170

Suggestions:

Celebrities make good role models:

1. They bring attention to issues that kids might normally ignore.
2. They show how kids can be just as talented as grownups.
3. Kids can aspire to be as successful as a celebrity.
4. Celebrity bad behavior can be a model for how NOT to be.
5. Some celebrities are well-behaved and good role models.

Celebrities make bad role models:

1. Many celebrities are famous for bad reasons (looks, being rich, etc.).
2. Celebrities sometimes model bad behavior.
3. Celebrities promote products that normal kids can't afford.
4. Many female celebrities starve themselves or get plastic surgery.

Q: Should Biggie Burger open?

First, READ the news story.

Protest at the New Biggie Burger

A crowd of kids and parents held signs and shouted outside the soon-to-be-opened Biggie Burger on Route 73. They were protesting because they don't want the new fast food restaurant to open. Ever.

"This kind of food is really bad for you!" said 12-year-old Diana Wong. "It's high in salt, fat, and sugar."

"Places like this bring strangers to the area," said Diana's mom. "And they take business away from our local restaurants."

Other locals disagree. The mayor insists that Biggie Burger will bring in much-needed tax dollars to help improve the town. And 17-year-old Sandi Corona can't wait for Biggie to open. "I love their fries! Plus, I can get a job there."

Sandi's dad, a construction worker, agrees, "Biggie's prices are just right for a family like ours."

As for Cyrus Matthews, who owns the guitar shop next door to Biggie Burger, he's excited too. "Maybe people who come for a Biggie Burger will swing by and check out my store."

The town will host a meeting on Thursday to hear both sides. Come by and voice your opinion!

READ each argument and FILL IN the supporting facts from the article.

ARGUMENT: ***YES! Biggie Burger should open.***

FACTS

1. The restaurant serves low-priced food.
2. ______________________________
3. ______________________________
4. ______________________________

ARGUMENT: ***NO! Biggie Burger should not open.***

FACTS

1. Fast food is high in salt, fat, and sugar.
2. ______________________________
3. ______________________________
4. ______________________________

Which argument has more facts to back it up?

Circle one: the YESes the NOs

What do YOU think? Should Biggie Burger open? Circle one: YES NO

Why or why not? ______________________________

____

You can agree with an argument, even if it has fewer facts supporting it.

Q: Should Paolo quit his soccer team?

First, READ Paolo's letter.

Dear Dad,

I know you've got lots to do with your army unit, but I'm hoping you can help me out anyway. See, I'm thinking of quitting the soccer team, and I want to know your opinion. Don't freak out!

It's just that my homework this year is crazy, and I need more time to get it done. Plus, since I'm the man of the house while you're gone, I've got a few extra chores.

On the other hand, I've put in two years on the team, and the coach says I'll make captain pretty soon. And, of course, I still LOVE soccer! It's way better than any other sport on Earth.

I'm a really good player (or so they tell me). But maybe I could try something new? I've been thinking about photography, actually. My soccer buds are great. We will be friends to the end, but it would be cool to meet some new kids.

What do you think, Dad?

Can't wait for you to come home!

Paolo

So? What do YOU think? Should Paolo quit the team?

FILL IN your argument and SUPPORT it with facts from Paolo's letter.

ARGUMENT

____

____

____

FACTS

Quit soccer

1. ______________________________
2. ______________________________
3. ______________________________
4. ______________________________
5. ______________________________

Stay on team

1. ______________________________
2. ______________________________
3. ______________________________
4. ______________________________
5. ______________________________

Q: Do celebrities make good role models?

First, READ the news story.

Star Spotlight

Lately it seems that young celebrities are making news more than ever before. But is it always bad news?

Thirteen-year-old Chyna Brewster has a poster of her favorite pop star, Stefanie Cruz, hanging on her wall. "I love her music!" she says. "Her songs are about real life—like my life!"

But Chyna's mom is worried. "That Cruz girl is always in the magazines, drinking and smoking. She's not even 18! I don't want my Chyna following in those footsteps."

Chyna laughs at her mom. "I know some kids who want to be famous like Stefanie one day. But I don't know anybody who wants to live her crazy life!"

Dr. Barney Webber, an expert on teenagers, agrees with Chyna's mom. "A lot of these young stars, like that rich party girl Athens Redroof, are famous for all the wrong reasons. Sometimes they're famous just for dating another famous person! That's nothing for kids to look up to. Especially when some young starlets starve themselves or get surgery just to look good."

Geoff Karzai, a 15-year-old skateboarder, says not all celebrities are the same. "Pro skater Dirk Handy came to town last week to help us raise money for a skate park. And, yeah, Athens Redroof sometimes drives on the wrong side of the road, but her boyfriend Jake Greatly visits our troops overseas. And a lot of kids I know talk about pollution because Jake talks about pollution."

"Besides," he adds, "when these stars act dumb, it just shows us how *not* to act, right?"

But Chyna's mom doesn't buy it. She won't buy their products either. "The stuff that these stars promote is way too expensive!" she says. "Last week, Chyna wanted a $1,000 purse that Lana Lonergan wore in her last movie. I told her she could buy it as soon as she earned as much money as Lana did."

Oswaldo Andrade plans to do just that. He and his band Taxicab are getting ready to play on *Star Hunt*, the reality TV show for young talent. "I don't care how a celebrity behaves offstage," says Oswaldo. "I think young stars prove that kids are just as talented as grownups."

No matter what, Chyna Brewster is going to keep her poster on the wall. But her head is in the right place. "When Stefanie Cruz gets in trouble, it's just something funny for my friends and me to talk about. No big deal!"

Make an Argument

So? What do YOU think? Do celebrities make good role models for kids?

FILL IN your argument and SUPPORT it with facts from the article.

ARGUMENT

____

____

____

FACTS

Celebrities make good role models.

1. ______________________________
2. ______________________________
3. ______________________________
4. ______________________________
5. ______________________________

Celebrities make bad role models.

1. ______________________________
2. ______________________________
3. ______________________________
4. ______________________________
5. ______________________________

When you're reading a nonfiction article or book, you should find out about the author. Why? Because the author's point of view on a topic shapes how he or she writes about it. A good reader keeps that in mind!

READ about this author.

Marvin Maxwell

Ever since he was a little boy, Marvin Maxwell wanted to be a jockey, and he learned how to ride a horse before he rode a bicycle. "There's nothing more exciting than watching horses race to the finish line. I was too tall to be a jockey, so I write about horses every chance I get."

1. CHECK the true statement.

☐ a. Marvin would think YES, it's right to race horses.

☐ b. Marvin would think NO, it's not right to race horses.

READ about this author.

Bettina Berkeley

Aliens have visited Bettina Berkeley her entire life. They've taken her to many galaxies and shown her their wonderful cities. This first-hand experience makes Bettina a major expert on extraterrestrial life. "Some people call me crazy," she says. "But they will soon know I'm right."

2. CHECK the true statement.

☐ a. Bettina would think YES, there's life on other planets.

☐ b. Bettina would think NO, there's no life on other planets.

Check It!

Page 171

1. a
2. a

Page 172

1. They are annoying because they interrupt his TV show.
2. He owns a candy store, so it might hurt his business.

Page 173

1. No
2. Magda wants Anna to stay in town with her to lifeguard, so she won't be alone.

Pages 174-175

Who Wrote This?

1. B
   Nathan is older and can't wait to get out of Littleboro. Story B seems to look down on younger kids and on Littleboro.
2. A
   Story A was all about the DJ music.
3. C
   Story C was all about the bands, and Derrick promotes bands.

Check It!

Pages 176-177

Who Wrote This?

1. C
   The author of story C was very proud of Middletown's athletics program, and Alma works for that program.
2. A
   The author of story A seems envious of Joel's success and acts like it wasn't really deserved. Tito has clearly been second place to Joel for a while.
3. B
   The author of story B is worried about Joel dropping out of school, and Hector is proud of the graduation rate.

Page 178

Suggestions:

1. Samoa would think that kids can stay up all night because she clearly stays up every night doing homework, and she loves coffee.
2. Lisa would say bedtime isn't important as long as kids get a lot of sleep because she loves to sleep.
3. Dr. Gilbert Blythe would say kids should go to bed early because he has a lot of kids but likes quiet time alone at night, and he wrote a book about kids getting lots of sleep.

Q: Should kids sell candy door to door?

First, READ the letter.

Dear Editor:

I don't know about you, but I am sick and tired of kids ringing my doorbell to sell me candy. They always seem to come right when my favorite TV show is on. So annoying! Sure, it's always for a "good cause," like jazz band or a trip to the aquarium, but why should I care? I think kid candy sellers should be stopped!

Yours truly,
Reginald Reynolds
Owner of the Candy Arcade on Main Street

Now, ANSWER the questions.

1. What reason does Reginald give for stopping kid candy sellers?

   ____

2. What's another reason that Reginald might want to stop kid candy sellers?

   ____

Do YOU think kids should sell candy door-to-door?

Circle one: YES NO

Why do you think that?

____

When you know an author's point of view, it helps you make up your OWN mind!

Q: What should Anna do this summer?

First, READ this letter.

Dear Anna,

As your best friend, I think it's very important that you have a great summer. So I decided to write you this letter and tell you exactly what you should do.

I know that your mom really wants you to take that babysitting gig with the Shahs at their lake house. That would be a major mistake! You hate lakes, and those Shah kids are total brats. Sure, at the end of the summer, you'd have a lot of money in the bank, but you'd be miserable!

Clearly you should spend the summer lifeguarding at the pool here in town. It's not as much money, but we would have so much fun! Every afternoon we could work on our tans and watch Kareem Singleton do his laps! There's not a lot going on here, but we'd have each other.

Summer only comes once a year. You don't want to mess it up.

XOXO,
Magda

P.S. No need to thank me for this advice. That's what friends are for!

Now, ANSWER the questions.

1. From her letter, do you think Magda is leaving town this summer?

   Circle one: YES NO

2. What do you think she wants Anna to do this summer? Why?

   ____

   ____

If you were Anna, would YOU stay in town? Circle one: YES NO Why?

____

Who Wrote This?

Can you match the story with the author? First, READ these stories.

A. Calling All Klub Kidz!

An exciting new business is coming to Littleboro. Klub Kidz! It's a place where kids ages 12 to 18 can mix and mingle to the beat of some great tunes. Unlike a grownup club, Klub Kidz will only serve soda, juice, and smoothies. And nobody over 18 is allowed on the dance floor!

The best part about the club is the music. The town's best young DJs will spin from 6 p.m. to 9 p.m. every night. The sound system is amazing: two turntables connected to speakers that surround the entire space. The club will play ska, hiphop, and other groovy sounds. Come on out and dance!

B. Korny Klub Kidz

In its latest attempt to be the corniest town on the planet, Littleboro will be opening a club for kids next week. And get this: it's called "Klub Kidz." Cute, huh? The club is painted with bright colors like a preschool, and there's a parent's lounge right next to the dance floor. The menu includes typical kid stuff: milk and cookies, peanut butter and jelly, etc. While it's aimed at kids ages 12 to 18, it's doubtful that anyone over the age of 14 would be caught dead there.

C. Finally, a Place for Local Music!

Attention all rock bands! If you're under 18, you'll finally have a chance to play some gigs. There's a new club coming to town called Klub Kidz. It's for kids ages 12 to 18. There's a dance floor and stage with a great sound system—perfect for live music! The club will feature two new bands every week, so start learning new songs!

Now, READ about these authors.

Nathan Gwirtz has been a regular teen critic for the *Littleboro Gazette* for three years. In the fall, he'll be attending Bigboro University as a freshman. He can't wait to leave small-town life behind.

1. Which Klub Kidz story do you think Nathan wrote? Circle one: A B C

   Why do you think that? ______________________________

   ____

"DJ Smooooth" (real name Ben Waldman) has been spinning records for parties all over Littleboro since he was ten years old. He was recently voted the best DJ at Littleboro Middle School, and he will be spinning tunes on opening night at Klub Kidz.

2. Which Klub Kidz story do you think DJ Smooooth wrote? Circle one: A B C

   Why do you think that? ______________________________

   ____

Derrick Zakaria, owner of Klub Kidz, has been promoting new clubs and bands in Littleboro for ten years. He hopes that his new club will attract all the best new talent, as well as kids that love to dance.

3. Which Klub Kidz story do you think Derrick wrote? Circle one: A B C

   Why do you think that? ______________________________

   ____

Who Wrote This?

Can you match the story with the author? First, READ these stories.

A. Going Pro at 16

It's every kid's dream: a career in professional sports. And now our own Joel Manheim will be living the dream. At only 16 years old, Manheim is joining one of the best basketball teams on the planet. Talk about being in the right place at the right time! The big-shot scouts happened to come to Joel's best game of the season. And, of course, a lot of his success has to do with knowing the right people. Still, we wish him the best of luck!

B. Free-Throwing Your Life Away

While most 16-year-olds will be sitting in class, Middletown resident Joel Manheim will be throwing a ball through a hoop. And earning millions of dollars!

But what if his NBA career falls through? Will he be just another high school dropout? Before he made it big, Joel was an A student, and class president. He would have been welcome at any college! One can only hope that his decision to leave the classroom behind won't harm him in years to come.

C. Chance of a Lifetime!

Everybody's talking about Joel Manheim. And why not? Joel is the product of Middletown's amazing athletic program. He's been playing ball in our gyms and on our fields since he was three years old. He lists three Middletown coaches as his main keys to success. We should be proud of our hometown hero!

Now, READ about these authors.

Alma Sakran, also known as "Coach," has been running Middletown's community athletics for 25 years. She's done it all: little league, soccer, basketball, and track. Her favorite part of her job is working with the kids and watching them grow.

1. Which Joel Manheim story do you think Alma wrote? Circle one: A B C

   Why do you think that? ______________________________

   ____

Tito Molinos, the new captain of Middletown High's basketball team, is the second highest scorer after Joel Manheim. He will probably be team MVP now that Joel has left to go pro.

2. Which Joel Manheim story do you think Tito wrote? Circle one: A B C

   Why do you think that? ______________________________

   ____

Hector Burgess has worked at Middletown High School as an English teacher for 20 years. He's proud to say that while he's been at the school, the percent of students to graduate has increased. Hector is also the advisor to the student council.

3. Which Joel Manheim story do you think Hector wrote? Circle one: A B C

   Why do you think that? ______________________________

   ____

Q: What time should kids go to bed?

READ about these authors and ANSWER the questions.

At twelve years old, **Samoa Klein** is the youngest student at Biggieburg University Law School. Her favorite possession is her coffee maker. She has at least eight hours of classes per day and does ten hours of homework each night. Her goal is to become a Supreme Court Justice by the time she's 30.

1. What do you think Samoa Klein would say about kids' bedtimes?

   ____

   Why do you think that? ______________________________

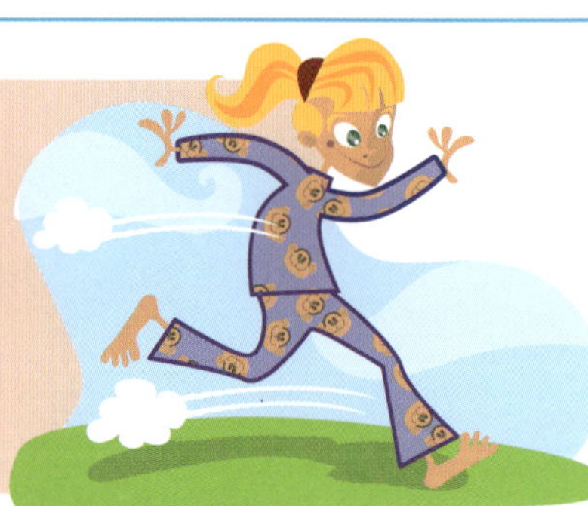

Biggieburg Junior track star **Lisa Hendrickson** is a record-breaking sprinter. Her key to success? "I take lots of naps." Lisa's favorite day of the week is Saturday because she can sleep all day. Her favorite outfit? "That would be my monkey pajamas!"

2. What do you think Lisa Hendrickson would say about kids' bedtimes?

   ____

   Why do you think that? ______________________________

A small town doctor for thirty years, **Dr. Gilbert Blythe** is also the father of seven children. He enjoys reading and spending quiet time alone at night. He has studied the effect of sleeplessness on children and wrote the book *Children at Rest Are Children at Their Best*.

3. What do you think Dr. Gilbert Blythe would say about kids' bedtimes?

   ____

   Why do you think that? ______________________________

How do you make sure all the information you read doesn't just slide out of your brain? You can make a chart, a diagram, or a timeline!

When you have a lot of events in a story or article, use a TIMELINE to put them in order.

Timeline

READ the article, then FILL IN the timeline.

Computers Then and Now

The first computers weren't for everybody. The Z3 was the first "real" computer, built in 1941 for use by the German government. In 1946, the U.S. Army got its ENIAC computer. (ENIAC is short for Electronic Numerical Integrator and Computer.) The ENIAC took up 1,000 square feet—the size of an apartment!

Thankfully *microprocessors* were invented in 1970, which made computers smaller and cheaper, so soon everyone could have one. In 1982, the Commodore 64 came out for $595. It became the best-selling personal computer of all time.

What happened in each of these years?

Year	Event
1941	____________
1946	____________
1970	____________
1982	____________

Check It!

Page 179

Timeline

Year	Event
1941	The first "real" computer was built.
1946	The ENIAC was built for the U.S. Army.
1970	The microprocessor was invented.
1982	The Commodore 64 came out for $595.

Page 180

Timeline

Time	Event
8:00	Mom told Jake she wasn't doing his laundry.
11:00	Jake broke the washing machine.
1:00	Jake dropped his lunch in the food court.
2:00	Stan Metz took Jake's bus pass.
2:30	Jake started walking home.
5:30	Jake got home, and Mom yelled.
8:00	Jake went to bed.

Page 181

Timeline

Day	Event	Winner
1	3-legged	The Rangers race (Cabin 1)
2	tug of war	Bugjuice (Cabin 2)
3	backward canoeing	Bugjuice (Cabin 2)
4	capture the flag	The Shooflies flag (Cabin 3)
5	obstacle course	The Rangers (Cabin 1)
6	water balloon toss	Bugjuice (Cabin 2)

Page 182

Diagram

Raging Rivers: Cannonball, movie theater
Flood Zone: lame Super Soaker, great minigolf, better food
Both: near home, great wave pools, same bumper boats

Page 183

Diagram

2 Wheels: don't need to push off, can do amazing turns, easy to ride, hard to stop, doesn't balance on its own, tiring
4 Wheels: have to push off to get going, jumps are better, guaranteed balance
Both: same length, same protective gear

Timeline

READ the story, then FILL IN the timeline.

Jake's Worst Day Ever!

By 1 o'clock, when I dropped my lunch in the food court, I knew this was the worst day ever. And it wasn't even halfway through! This evil day started at 8 a.m., when Mom told me she was "on strike" and wasn't doing my laundry anymore. By 11, I was up to my knees in the soapy water that was bubbling out of the washing machine. I ran away to the mall for some peace (and lunch). At 2 p.m., Stan Metz and his barfy friends were stealing my bus pass. It took me three hours to walk home! And when I got there at 5:30, Mom was on the warpath. She screamed at me for an hour! Needless to say, I went to bed at 8 p.m., without dinner. Maybe tomorrow will be better!

What was happening to Jake at each of these times?

Time	Event
8:00	mom is on strike won't do my laundry eny[illegible]
11:00	on kness in soapy water that came out of w[illegible]
1:00	i dropped my lunch off in food cart
2:00	
2:30	
5:30	
8:00	

Check It!

Page 184

Diagram

Sumo: touch floor with one part of body, can use legs, rice-straw mat, wear a *mawashi*, not in the Olympics, no shoes
Greco-Roman: touch floor with three parts, rubber mat, wear a singlet, wear shoes, in the Olympics
Both: must touch the floor to lose, stepping out of bounds is bad, play inside a circle, play on a mat

Page 185

Chart

Animal	Home	Food
Aye-Aye	Madagascar	grubs
Quokka	Australia	grasses
Capybara	South America	grasses

Pages 186-187

Chart

Roller Coaster	Height/ Length	Speed	Duration
Top Thrill Dragster	420'/ 2,800'	120 mph	17 sec
Kingda Ka	456'/ 3,118'	128 mph	28 sec
Steel Dragon 2000	318'/ 8,133'	95 mph	4 min
Tower of Terror	377'/ 1,235'	100 mph	28 sec

1. Kingda Ka
2. Kingda Ka
3. Steel Dragon 2000
4. Steel Dragon 2000

Page 188

Chart

Name	Team	Color
Ariel	Soaker	red
Raja	Drencher	blue
Nora	Drencher	purple
Ben	Drencher	yellow
Jeremy	Soaker	orange
Sofia	Soaker	green

Timeline

READ the story, then FILL IN the timeline.

Cabin Combat

Camp Kiki's 5-Day Cabin Combat was a major success! All three teams fought hard to win each day's event. The Shooflies from Cabin Three had a rough time of it. They lost for the first three days, finally capturing a win in the capture the flag game. Too bad that was their only win!

Cabin One's Rangers and Cabin Two's Bugjuice were neck and neck the whole time. The Rangers scored the first win of the games when their team crossed the finish line during the three-legged race. Then Bugjuice took the crown on day two after easily winning the tug of war. They also won the next day, showing their amazing skills at backward canoeing. All eyes turned to the final event: the obstacle course. Would the Rangers be able to tie up the score? They did! The games went into an extra day. The tie-breaker event was the water balloon toss. You could cut the tension with a knife! After tossing for nearly half an hour, the Rangers let it drop—*splash!* Congratulations, Bugjuice!

What happened each day during the 5-Day Cabin Combat?

Day	Event	Winner
1		
2		
3		
4		
5		
6		

Diagram

If you're reading a story that's comparing two or three subjects, use a DIAGRAM to keep it straight!

READ the story, then FILL IN the blanks.

Splish-Splash Clash!

My twin sister Darla and I can't agree on which water park to go to for our birthday. Both Raging Rivers and Flood Zone are close to our town. My sister likes Flood Zone better. How can she be so wrong? I tried to tell her that Raging Rivers has great thrill rides, like the Cannonball, which drops you over fifty feet! And my favorite thing about Raging Rivers is the movie theater. You can sit in the water and watch a fun 3-D movie! Flood Zone doesn't have that.

Flood Zone has lame rides like the Super Soaker, which is for babies. Both parks have great wave pools, and their bumper boats are pretty much the same. But Darla likes minigolf, and Flood Zone has great courses. They also have better food, I'll admit that. But you don't go to water parks to eat!

It's too bad we can't take both parks and mush them into one!

Raging Rivers	Both	Flood Zone
__________	__________	__________
__________	__________	__________
	__________	__________

Diagram

READ the article, then FILL IN the blanks.

Street Surfing

For most of its history, the skateboard rolled along on four wheels. But not anymore! Newer models feature only two wheels with a springy middle that allows riders to "surf" along by twisting with their feet and legs. On a traditional four-wheel board, the rider has to keep pushing off from the pavement in order to get some speed. You don't need to keep pushing a two-wheeler!

The two wheels spin around, so you can do amazing turns, but jumps still work better on a four-wheeler. The two-wheel board is easy to ride but hard to stop because it doesn't balance on its own. It also wipes you out! Your muscles will be sore by the end of the block. The newer board is about the same length as a longer four-wheel board, and you'll need the same kind of protective gear.

If you want guaranteed balance, stick with four wheels. But for an easy, smooth ride and tight turns, drop some wheels and catch the wave!

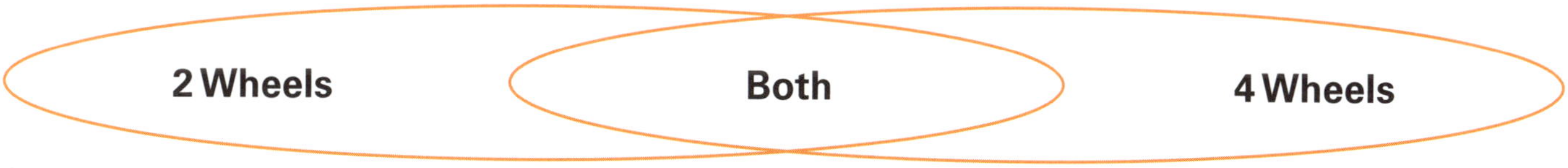

2 Wheels	Both	4 Wheels
________________	________________	________________
________________	________________	________________
________________		________________
________________		
________________		
________________		

Diagram

READ the article, then FILL IN the blanks.

Wrestling Two Ways

If you've watched the Olympics, you may have seen Greco-Roman wrestling. But have you ever seen sumo wrestling? Sumo is the ancient (and very popular) art of wrestling in Japan.

The goal of both wrestlers is the same: They want to get their opponents to touch the floor or step out of bounds. In sumo, a losing wrestler only has to touch the floor with any single part of his body (except his feet). A Greco-Roman wrestler must touch with three parts of his body in order to lose a match. In both sports, stepping out of bounds is a losing move. Sumo wrestlers can use their legs to trip their opponents. Greco-Roman wrestlers aren't allowed to use their legs.

Both kinds of wrestlers compete inside a circle drawn on a mat. In the case of Greco-Roman wrestling, the mat is made of rubber. Sumo wrestlers compete on a *dohyo*, a mat of rice-straw bales. Greco-Roman wrestlers wear a *singlet*, which is a tight bodysuit designed to keep wrestlers from grabbing hold of each other's outfit. On the other hand, a sumo wrestler's *mawashi* can legally be used to grab and throw a wrestler out of the ring. Greco-Roman wrestlers also wear shoes during a match, while sumo wrestlers compete barefoot.

Sumo isn't an Olympic sport—yet! But keep your eye out for it.

Sumo	Both	Greco-Roman
______	______	______
______	______	______
______	______	______
______	______	______
______		______
______		

Chart

If what you're reading has a lot of characteristics or details to follow, try using a CHART to keep things straight!

READ the story, then FILL IN the chart.

Whacky Animals

Have you ever heard of an aye-aye? That's a little, bug-eyed animal that lives in Madagascar. It loves yummy grubs, and it has a long, skinny middle finger that it uses to dig them out of tree trunks. How about the quokka? It's a marsupial from Australia, with a front pouch like a kangaroo. It chomps on grasses and isn't at all afraid of humans. (But don't feed the quokkas!) Okay, try this one: capybara. Sound familiar? It's the largest rodent in the world—imagine a four foot long squirrel (without a tail). Like the quokka, the capybara chows down on grasses. It lives in South America.

FILL IN the chart with the information from the story.

Animal	Home	Food
Aye-Aye		
Quokka		
Capybara		

Isn't the chart easier to read? Keep going!

Chart

READ the article, then FILL IN the chart on the next page.

Roller Coaster Ups & Downs

When you're comparing roller coasters, you should look at how tall they are (their *height*), how long they are (their *length*), and how fast they go. Let's see how some popular steel roller coasters measure up!

Cedar Point, in Ohio, has the most roller coasters. The Top Thrill Dragster is 420 feet high and 2,800 feet long. Kingda Ka, at Six Flags Great Adventure in New Jersey, is 456 feet tall, 3,118 feet long, and it goes up to 128 miles per hour (mph). That's faster than Top Thrill Dragster, which only gets up to 120 mph. The Steel Dragon 2000 in Japan is 318 feet tall, 8,133 feet long, and goes 95 mph. The Tower of Terror in Australia is 377 feet tall, 1,235 feet long, and goes up to 100 mph.

You can also look at how long the ride lasts (*duration*). The longer the better, right? Well, when you're going this fast, you can't expect a long ride. The Top Thrill Dragster lasts 17 seconds. Kingda Ka and Tower of Terror will both thrill you for 28 seconds. Steel Dragon 2000 gives you four minutes of fun.

Which ride is the best? You be the judge!

FILL IN the chart with the information from the article.

Roller Coaster	Height/Length	Speed	Duration

Now, use your chart to answer these questions.

1. Which is the fastest coaster?

____

2. Which is the tallest coaster?

____

3. Which is the longest coaster?

____

4. Which ride lasts the longest?

____

Did you use the article or the chart to answer these questions? _______________

Chart

READ the story, then FILL IN the chart.

HINT: Read carefully to figure out all the clues!

High Noon on Haddock Street

Let the battle begin! One hot Tuesday afternoon, the kids on Haddock Street filled up their balloons and teamed up to fight a water war. The two teams were the Soakers and the Drenchers. Each of the six kids had their own color of balloon. For instance, Ariel (Soaker) used red balloons. Her brother Raja (Drencher) threw blue ones. (Only a member of Drenchers team threw purple balloons.)

The kids played until each one of them got hit. No player hit a member of the same team. Nora got soaked by a Soaker's green balloon. Ben (who threw yellow balloons) was blasted by a red balloon.

The Drenchers team had two boys and one girl. The Soakers had two girls and one boy. Jeremy was a Soaker. He threw orange balloons. Poor Sofia got hit early on. She only used one of her balloons—to hit Nora.

FILL IN the information you got from the story.

Name	Team	Color

Another way to track information in a story is to map it! For a fictional story, your STORY MAP should include the characters, the setting, the problem, and the solution.

Story Map

READ the story, then FILL IN the story map.

Little Red

Once there was this girl whom everyone called "Little Red" because she wore red clothes all the time. One day, Little Red headed out to visit her grandma on the other side of the big city. When she got to her grandma's apartment, Little Red immediately noticed something wasn't right. First of all, her grandma looked a lot hairier than usual. Second of all, her grandma looked a lot toothier than usual. Third of all, her grandma looked a LOT wolfier than usual! Little Red used her cell phone to call the police. They found her grandma tied up in the closet. "Silly wolf!" said Little Red, as they put him in jail. "You can't fool me."

Characters

____

____

____

Problem

____

____

____

Title

____

Solution

____

____

____

Setting

____

____

____

Check It!

Page 189

Story Map

Title: Little Red
Characters: Little Red, wolf, grandma
Setting: the big city, grandma's apartment
Problem: Grandma seems strange.
Solution: Little Red calls the police on her cell phone.

Page 190

Story Map

Title: Stinkerbell
Characters: Taj, Stinkerbell, Taj's mom
Setting: house and farm
Problem: Stinkerbell cannot be housebroken.
Solution: They brought Stinkerbell to the farm.

Page 191

Story Map

Title: Just for Kicks
Characters: Theresa, Theresa's mom
Setting: the beach
Problem: Theresa has a secret.
Solution: Theresa decides to tell her mom.

Pages 192-193

Story Map

Title: Mall Rats
Characters: Luke, Vin, and Zeke
Setting: the mall
Problem: Zombie mall rats
Solution: cinnamon buns

Story Map

READ the story, then FILL IN the story map.

Stinkerbell

Taj woke up to find a puppy licking his toes. What a great birthday gift! He named his new best friend Stinkerbell.

The little puppy lived up to her name. She made messes in every corner of Taj's house. She ran away every chance she got. She chewed everything that would fit in her mouth.

Taj tried to teach her, but Stinkerbell wouldn't listen.

"She's just an outdoor dog," said Taj's mom.

One day, they drove Stinkerbell to a farm at the edge of town. She jumped out of the car and ran in circles, barking and wagging like crazy.

"I think she'll be happy here," said Taj, wiping a tear from his cheek.

Characters

______

______

______

Problem

______

______

______

Title

______

Solution

______

______

______

Setting

______

______

Check It!

Page 194

Mind Map

Main Idea: Freaky Speed Records

Details:

1. lawn mower race
2. motorized sofa
3. fastest walk on water
4. fastest walk on hands

Pages 195-196

Mind Map

Big Idea: Silly Sports

In the Water:

1. bog snorkeling
2. Octopush

In the Backyard:

1. cheese rolling
2. toe wrestling
3. Zorb

In a Stadium:

1. chessboxing
2. fistball

Story Map

READ the story, then FILL IN the story map.

Just for Kicks

It was a beautiful summer day at the beach, but Theresa didn't care. She was carrying a secret that felt like a one-ton weight in the middle of her stomach.

Any minute now, she thought, they'll find out and I'll be in trouble. So far, nobody knew. And that was worse! She kicked herself for listening to Sharice.

"It'll be fun," her friend had said. "We'll do it just for kicks."

So here she was, at the beach with her family, miserable. If only she could tell!

Suddenly her mother put an arm around her. "What's wrong, Tee?" she asked. "You look down in the dumps."

Theresa looked up into her mother's eyes. Maybe she COULD tell!

"Mom," she said, "Sharice and I broke a window in the old Lombard house. Just for kicks."

Sure, Mom was mad. Playing in empty houses isn't safe. It also happens to be illegal. Theresa was in big trouble. Even so, Theresa smiled and began to enjoy the sun and the sand. Even getting in trouble felt better than that secret!

	Characters __________ __________	
Problem __________ __________	Title __________ __________	Solution __________ __________
	Setting __________ __________	

Story Map

READ the story.

Mall Rats

Zeke and Vin were surrounded. Just when they thought they were goners, Luke dangled a rope from the ceiling of the skate store. "Grab it!" he yelled.

They grabbed, of course. As they climbed up, the rats below tried to jump up onto their legs, but the boys kicked them off.

Mall rats. The worst kind there is. And these were zombies, so you couldn't kill them. Luke, Zeke, and Vin had gone to the mall to hang out three days ago. Now they were climbing in the ceiling above the stores and camping in the camping supply shop.

And they were the lucky ones.

Vin had an idea. He was always the man with the plan. But would it work?

The next day, the boys climbed to the food court. Below them, the cinnamon bun place should have been packed on a Saturday. But it was empty. There were lots of buns sitting in the glass case. Vin lowered himself down to the case and opened the doors. He threw all the cinnamon buns out into the middle of the food court.

The rats took the bait. Every single one of them zipped into the food court and started chowing down on the sticky-sweet treats.

"Let's get out of here!" hollered Vin. He and the others raced for the door.

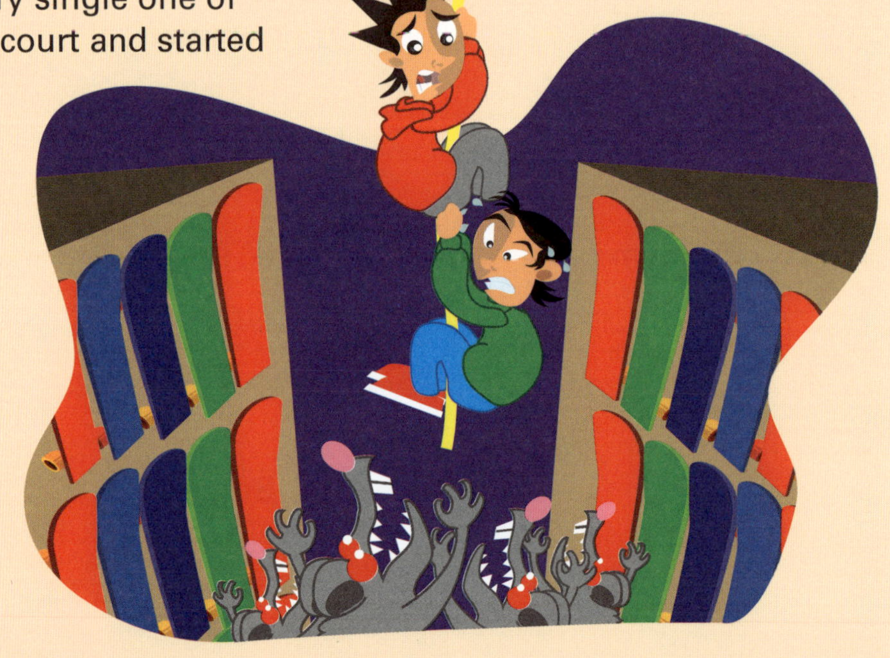

FILL IN the story map.

	Characters	
Problem	Title	Solution
	Setting	

What was your favorite part of the story?

What do you think happened to the boys next?

Mind Map

When you're reading a nonfiction story, use a MIND MAP to keep track of the main ideas and the details.

READ the story, then FILL IN the mind map.

Fast and Freaky

Want to break a speed record? Hop on your lawn mower and let's go! In England, they've been racing lawn mowers since 1973. During the 12-hour race, the farthest anyone's ever gone is 313.6 miles. That's only 26 miles per hour. Let's try the couch next. One couch potato made a motorized sofa that can go 87 mph. Prefer to walk? A Frenchman walked all the way across the Atlantic Ocean on special ski floats. It took two months. Or you could follow in Johann Hurlinger's footsteps—or handsteps. Johann walked 870 miles on his hands! It took 55 days at about 1.58 miles per hour.

Like they say, it's not where you're going, it's how you get there!

Freaky Speed Records

Main Idea

1. ______________________

2. ______________________

3. ______________________

4. ______________________

Mind Map

READ the story, then FILL IN the mind map on the next page.

Silly Sports

Do football, baseball, and basketball make you yawn? Well, the world is filled with wild and wacky games you can play in the water, your backyard, or a big stadium.

Grab your snorkel and head to the nearest bog. What's a bog? It's a muddy, smelly bit of swamp. Every year, a village in Wales makes a 200-foot trench in a bog, and people swim two laps, breathing through their snorkel tubes. Or if that doesn't suit you, try a game called Octopush. It's like hockey played at the bottom of a swimming pool, with a puck and tiny hockey sticks. Players breathe through snorkels during the game.

If you prefer to play outside, try cheese rolling. Start at the top of the hill with a big, round, hunk of cheese. Drop the cheese, then chase it. If you can catch the cheese before you get to the bottom, you win. Then there's toe wrestling (like thumb wrestling but using toes instead). But the craziest game of all may be Zorb. To play Zorb, simply get inside a giant, clear plastic ball (like a hamster ball). Start rolling!

If you can fill a stadium with crowds of fans, you should try chessboxing. In chessboxing, players alternate between playing chess and punching each other in the face. But if you don't like either chess or boxing, then that's not the sport for you. Try fistball instead! Like in volleyball, fistballers punch a ball back and forth across a net, using their fists instead of palms. Fistball is a really old sport, dating back to 1555, and it's played all over the world!

Now pick a sport and start training!

TURN the page and FILL IN the mind map.

Make a Map

FILL IN the mind map.

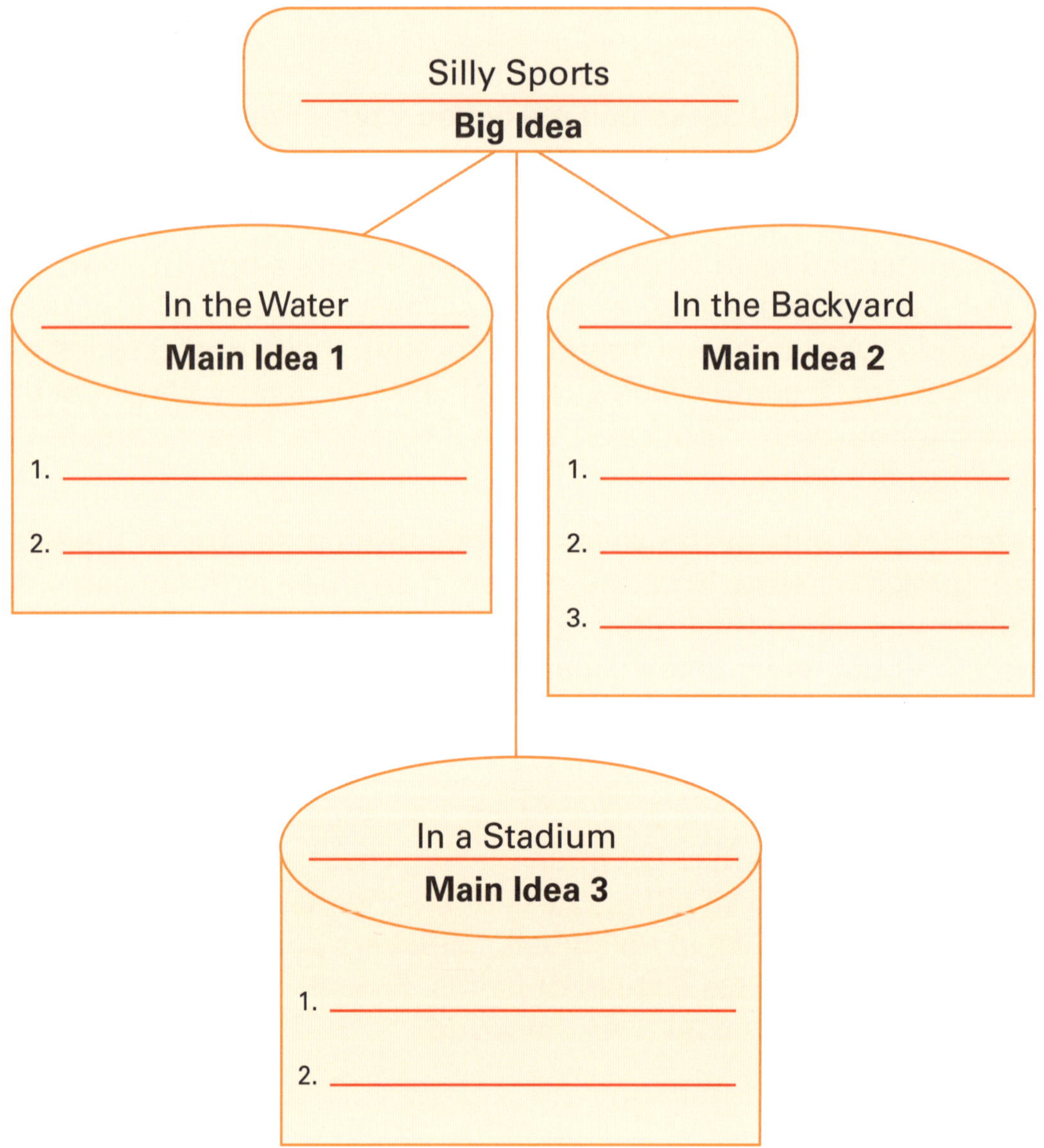

5th-Grade Writing Success

Fact and Fiction

Some people love to write. Some people hate it. No matter how you feel, writing is the best way for you to share all those big ideas in your head. And the world needs your big ideas!

When you stick to the facts, that's NONFICTION. You always have to tell the truth and check your information when you write this kind of story.

FILL IN the blanks with fiction and nonfiction story ideas for each topic.

Topic: Sharks

Fact: A shark attack survivor telling his terrible story

Fiction: A girl getting a pet shark and keeping it in her bathtub

Topic: Baseball

Fact: ______________________________

Fiction: ______________________________

Topic: Outer Space

Fact: ______________________________

Fiction: ______________________________

Topic: Rock 'n' Roll Music

Fact: ______________________________

Fiction: ______________________________

Actually, you can write *exactly* the *same* stories for both fiction and nonfiction, but in nonfiction, every word has to be true.

Check It!

Page 199

Fact and Fiction

Suggestions:

Topic: Baseball
Fact: The Red Sox winning the World Series
Fiction: A 10-year-old who joins the major leagues

Topic: Outer Space
Fact: The moons of Jupiter
Fiction: A kid who moves to Jupiter with his family

Topic: Rock 'n' Roll Music
Fact: A real-life band on their first worldwide tour
Fiction: A made-up story about a kid who starts a band with his parents

Page 200

Suggestions:

1. Shirley Temple
2. Amelia Earhart
3. George Clooney
4. Franklin D. Roosevelt
5. Marie Curie

Page 201

Suggestions:

1. the sun
2. the 1920s
3. industrial farming
4. global warming
5. the Civil War

Page 202

Suggestions:

1. make a paper airplane
2. make paper flowers
3. braid hair
4. roller blade
5. do a lay-up

Check It!

Page 203

Suggestions:

1. Reggie Jackson joining the Yankees
2. Surviving the *Titanic* disaster
3. The U.S. hockey team win at the 1980 Olympics
4. Charles Lindbergh's first nonstop flight from New York to Paris
5. The Brooklyn Dodgers move to Los Angeles

Page 204

Suggestions:

1. **Go:**
   - A ski resort, like Big Sky in Montana
   - A local snowboarding supply store
   - A snowboarding club meeting or class

2. **Read:**
   - Magazines for snowboarders
   - Books about snowboarding
   - A snowboarding blog on the Internet

3. **Ask:**
   - An expert snowboarder
   - A snowboard supply specialist
   - A reporter who covers snowboarding competitions

You can write nonfiction stories about tons of different topics, like people, history, nature, and sports. These topics are called GENRES.

When you write a story about a person's life, it's called a *biography*. When you write your own life story, that's an *autobiography*.

READ this story.

Boy on a Board

Tony Hawk got his first skateboard when he was nine years old. Before that, he says, "I was a hyper, rail-thin geek on a sugar buzz." That skateboard changed everything. As he got good at skating, he calmed down, felt better about himself, and thought more about other people. He really started to grow up.

Now, LIST five people you would like to write nonfiction stories about.

1. ______________________

2. ______________________

3. ______________________

4. ______________________

5. ______________________

You can also write about science or history to help your readers learn about those topics.

READ these stories.

On the Job at Five

During the Industrial Revolution in the 1800s, factory workers spent 16 hours straight in hot, smelly rooms filled with loud and dangerous machines. A lot of these workers were kids—some as young as five years old. Children were really useful because they had small fingers that could make tiny things like matches or nails. They could also fit inside the chimneys of rich people's houses to clean them.

These kids were helping to support their families, but most adults didn't like the idea. Over time, the government stepped in. Most countries made it illegal for people under the age of about 14 to have a job. However, "most" countries doesn't mean *all* countries. There are some places where little kids still spend their days sewing, farming, or working in factories.

Rotating with Earth

The Earth is rotating under our feet. It's traveling west to east at about 500 miles per hour. So why can't you just go up in a helicopter, hover in one spot for a few hours, and then land in a totally different place? (No, it doesn't work.) See, the Earth takes its atmosphere along for the ride. If it didn't, we'd be in trouble. Imagine a dog hanging its head out of a car window while the car is driving 500 miles per hour down the road!

Now, LIST five history, science, or nature topics you would like to write nonfiction stories about.

1. ______________________________

2. ______________________________

3. ______________________________

4. ______________________________

5. ______________________________

Do you know how to do something really well? Can you teach other people how to do it? That's another genre: instructional writing or "how-to."

READ this story.

How to Fly a Paper Helicopter

What you'll need:
- Paper or cardboard
- 1 paper clip
- Scissors

It's easy to make a helicopter.

Step 1: Cut a strip of cardboard or heavy paper that's 1 inch wide and 11 inches long.

Step 2: From one end of the strip, make a cut halfway through to the middle of the strip. This part will be the wings.

Step 3: Put your scissors about a half inch below the wings and make a small cut in toward the middle from both sides. (Don't cut all the way through.) This will be the body of your helicopter.

Step 4: Fold the sides of the body in so that it's kind of skinny.

Step 5: Then fold up the end of the body and slip on a paper clip.

Step 6: Fold the wings down in two different directions, so that they split and look like the top of a *Y*.

Step 7: Time to fly! Hold your helicopter by the paper clip and throw it up as high as you can. It should come spinning down, just like a whirly-bird.

LIST five things you could teach people to do.

1. ______________________________

2. ______________________________

3. ______________________________

4. ______________________________

5. ______________________________

Nonfiction doesn't mean boring—in fact, no writing should be boring. Sports and adventure are nonfiction genres too. And there's nothing boring about them!

READ this story.

Ship versus Ice

The *Endurance* was well named. She was a strong ship, built to withstand the crushing impact of the ice in the seas around Antarctica. Throughout the winter, she was frozen, locked in the ice that had grown until there was no more sea except deep below. Even then, *Endurance* lived up to her name. Then came spring. The air became a little warmer, the ice began to break, and the crew began to hope. Yes, the ice broke. It moved, it bucked, and it slammed. The huge ice floes were more dangerous as they wakened from their winter slumber and broke apart. *Endurance* couldn't take the punishment. Her hull splintered. The water poured in. The crew packed up their things, and carried their lifeboats with them down onto the ice floes. They could still walk for miles on the frozen, moving sea.

LIST five real-life adventures or true sports stories you'd like to write about.

1. ____________________

2. ____________________

3. ____________________

4. ____________________

5. ____________________

Writing Nonfiction

Since nonfiction is all about facts, you really need to know your stuff. In other words, you need to RESEARCH your topic.

There are three ways to research a topic:

1. You can go someplace and see something (like a museum).
2. You can read something (like a magazine article).
3. You can ask someone (like an expert).

FILL IN the blanks.

Topic: Snowboarding

1. Where could you go to research snowboarding?

____

____

____

2. What could you read about snowboarding?

____

____

____

3. Who could you ask about snowboarding?

____

____

____

Cut out the Check It! section on page 199, and see if you got the answers right. Then you'll be ready to start writing.

Bio Interview

For a biography, the best research you can do is to interview the person you want to write about.

LIST five questions you would ask someone to write their biography. Then find someone to ask, or ask yourself. FILL IN the answers.

1. Question: ______________________________

____

Answer: ______________________________

____

____

2. Question: ______________________________

____

Answer: ______________________________

____

____

3. Question: ______________________________

____

Answer: ______________________________

____

____

4. Question: ______________________________

____

Answer: ______________________________

____

____

Author! Author!

Now it's your turn. WRITE a short biography (or autobiography) based on the interview you did on the last page.

You've seen how many nonfiction topics you can write about. Now it's time to make a choice. Look back over your ideas from pages 200 through 203. Pick your favorites and think of some more.

LIST five nonfiction topics that you might want to write about.

1. ______________________________

2. ______________________________

3. ______________________________

4. ______________________________

5. ______________________________

Now, WRITE your favorite genre.

____

Check It!

Page 208

Pizza Topic Suggestions:
- How pizza came to America
- The best pizza in town
- Pizza world records
- Pizza all over the world

Dinosaur Topic Suggestions:
- Vegetarian dinosaurs
- Biggest dinosaurs
- Humans in the time of dinosaurs
- Digging up dinosaur bones
- Where dinosaurs lived

Pages 210-211

1. Famous athletes
2. New York City
3. Piano lessons
4. Aliens: fact and fiction
5. Riding a skateboard
6. Castles
7. Professional wrestlers
8. Playground games
9. Killer whales
10. Music from around the world
11. Animals of Australia
12. Crazy world records

Page 212

1. b
2. a
3. b
4. a

Pages 213-214

Suggestions:
1. When it comes to ice cream, there are way more than thirty-one flavors out there.
2. Early bedtimes for weekdays might make sense, but on the weekend, bedtimes should be much later.
3. Before you head out to the beach this summer, make sure you've got everything you need.
4. Planning a party? Here are some great ideas.
5. Everyone knows the best kind of pet is a cat. Here's why.
6. Siblings can be a total pain, but you know deep down you love them, right?
7. Don't let a little rain get you down. There's plenty of stuff to do indoors.
8. Next time you see a buzzing bee, take a closer look.
9. Some sports were meant to be played, not watched.

Wait a minute! Are any of your topics too big for a one-page story? For example, the topic of "pizza" is just too big. Let's break it down.

LIST five smaller topics that fit under the big topic of pizza.

Pizza Topics:

My favorite toppings

Try it again, this time with dinosaurs.

Dinosaur Topics:

Tyrannosaurus Rex

Now, GO BACK to your topic list on page 207. PICK two of your topics and break them into smaller topics.

Big Topic:

____

Small Topic:

____

____

____

____

____

Big Topic:

____

Small Topic:

____

____

____

____

____

Don't forget about research. Pick a topic that you know a lot about, or that you want to learn more about.

Which of these topics do you know the most about?

____

Which of these topics would you like to learn more about?

____

So, which topic do you most want to write about?

____

Congratulations—you've picked a topic!

Topic & Topic Sentence

Your readers need to know your topic right away. They get it from your TOPIC SENTENCE. That's usually the first sentence (or two) of your story.

READ each topic sentence. Then, FILL IN the blanks with the right topics from the box.

Topics

Animals of Australia
Crazy world records
Castles
New York City
Riding a skateboard
Famous athletes
Music from around the world
Playground games
Killer whales
Aliens: fact and fiction
Professional wrestlers
Piano lessons

1. **Topic:** ________________________________

   Sentence: Some sports stars are known all over the world.

2. **Topic:** ________________________________

   Sentence: The Big Apple. Gotham City. The largest city in the United States goes by many names.

3. **Topic:** ________________________________

   Sentence: If you think learning to play scales is a waste of time, think again.

4. **Topic:** ________________________________

   Sentence: When it comes to life in outer space, it's important to separate the truth from the tall tales.

EARTH

5. **Topic:** ______________________

Sentence: There's no better way to cruise down the sidewalk than on four wheels and a board.

6. **Topic:** ______________________

Sentence: Kings and queens sure know how to live large, in houses fit for royalty.

7. **Topic:** ______________________

Sentence: Behind their masks and wild behavior, most professional wrestlers are real athletes.

8. **Topic:** ______________________

Sentence: From kickball to four square, some of the best games come from the playground.

9. **Topic:** ______________________

Sentence: The first thing you need to know about killer whales is that they're actually dolphins.

10. **Topic:** ______________________

Sentence: People from every nation groove to their own special beat.

11. **Topic:** ______________________

Sentence: From kangaroos to quokkas, Australia is home to many interesting animals.

12. **Topic:** ______________________

Sentence: Some people will do anything to set a world record.

Topic & Topic Sentence

A good topic sentence doesn't just say what the story is about. It grabs the reader's attention. Don't be a boring writer. A bored reader usually stops reading.

READ the topic sentences below. CHECK the ones that are *not* boring.

1. **Topic: Hershey's Chocolate**

   ☐ a. The Hershey Chocolate Company was started in 1894 in Derry Church, PA (now called Hershey, PA).

   ☐ b. Hershey bars are so big they named a town after them.

2. **Topic: Charlie Chaplin**

   ☐ a. Charlie Chaplin packed a lot of living into his 77 years.

   ☐ b. Charlie Chaplin lived to be 77 years old. He made more than 90 movies, won three Academy Awards, wrote hundreds of songs, and was married three times.

3. **Topic: Prairie Dogs**

   ☐ a. Prairie dogs are a type of squirrel and bark when they sense danger.

   ☐ b. What do you call a squirrel that barks? A prairie dog, that's what!

4. **Topic: The History of Basketball**

   ☐ a. Believe it or not, the first basketball game was played with a soccer ball and a peach basket.

   ☐ b. The game of basketball was invented in 1891. The first players used a peach basket for a hoop and a soccer ball.

Now it's your turn. WRITE a topic sentence (or two) for each of these topics.

HINT: Don't worry if you only know a little about the topic.

1. **Topic: Ice cream flavors**

____

____

2. **Topic: Weekend bedtimes**

____

____

3. **Topic: Things to bring when you go to the beach**

____

____

4. **Topic: Great party ideas**

____

____

5. **Topic: The best kind of pets**

____

____

6. **Topic: Brothers and sisters**

7. **Topic: Things to do on a rainy day**

8. **Topic: Bees**

9. **Topic: Sports that are boring to watch on TV**

Finally, WRITE the topic sentence for the topic you picked on page 209.

Cut out the Check It! section on page 207, and see if you got the answers right.

Now that you have a topic and a topic sentence, how do you fill the rest of the page? Easy! Just use MAIN IDEAS and DETAILS. You'll need to MAP them out before you write. FILL IN the blanks with supporting details from the box.

Topic: Birds

Details

parakeets	worms	songbirds	birds of prey
cockatoos	waterbirds	small animals	
fruit	budgerigars	seeds	

Main Ideas

Types of Birds

1. ____________
2. ____________
3. ____________

Bird Food

1. ____________
2. ____________
3. ____________
4. ____________

Bird Pets

1. ____________
2. ____________
3. ____________

When you map out your story, you start with your main ideas, and you support them with details.

Check It!

Page 215

Types of Birds: water birds, songbirds, birds of prey
Bird Food: worms, seeds, small animals, fruit
Bird Pets: parakeets, cockatoos, budgerigars

Pages 216-217

Main Idea 1: What's a snail?
Supporting Details:
1. Snails are mollusks.
2. Mollusks are animals with no bones.
3. A snail without a shell is called a *slug*.

Main Idea 2: Snail description
Supporting Details:
1. Snails are about 1.5 inches long.
2. Some snails have spiral-shaped shells.
3. Some snails have eyes on the end of tentacles.

Main Idea 3: How snails move
Supporting Details:
1. Snails glide along using one muscular foot.
2. They only go about 1 mm per second.
3. They use mucus to slide and avoid injury.

Main Idea 4: Snails and food
Supporting Details:
1. Snails eat fruits and vegetables.
2. People eat snails.
3. In France, a dish of snails is called *escargot*.

Before you write a nonfiction story, you should MAP it.

FILL IN the nonfiction story map on the next page with the main ideas and details in the list.

Topic: Snails

Some have spiral-shaped shells.

Snails and food

Mollusks are animals with no bones.

In France, a dish of snails is called *escargot*.

Some snails have eyes on the end of tentacles.

What's a snail?

Snails glide along using one muscular foot.

A snail is a mollusk.

A snail without a shell is called a *slug*.

Snail description

Snails are about 1.5 inches long.

Snails use mucus to slide and avoid injury while moving.

People eat snails.

How snails move

Snails eat mostly fruits and vegetables.

Snails travel at speeds of about 1 millimeter per second.

Check It!

Page 218

Details suggestions:
Hamburgers
French fries
Fried chicken
McDonald's
Wendy's
Burger King
High fat content
High sugar content in soda
High salt content
Drive-through windows
Premade food
Quick ordering process

Main Ideas suggestions:
Fast food restaurants
Kinds of fast food
Fast food is bad for you.
Fast food is FAST.

Topic Sentence Suggestion:
Americans like their food, and they like it FAST.

Page 219

Suggestions:
Topic sentence: Americans like their food, and they like it FAST!

Main Idea 1: Kinds of fast food
Supporting Details:
1. Hamburgers
2. French fries
3. Fried chicken

Main Idea 2: Fast food restaurants
Supporting Details:
1. McDonald's
2. Wendy's
3. Burger King

Main Idea 3: Fast food is FAST.
Supporting Details:
1. Premade food
2. Quick ordering process
3. Drive-through windows

Main Idea 4: Fast food is bad for you.
Supporting Details:
1. High fat content
2. High salt content
3. High sugar content in sodas

Topic: Snails

Topic Sentence
Believe it or not, a snail is an animal, not a bug.

Paragraph 1. Main Idea

____

____

Supporting Details

1. ______________________________
2. ______________________________
3. ______________________________

Paragraph 2. Main Idea

____

____

Supporting Details

1. ______________________________
2. ______________________________
3. ______________________________

Paragraph 3. Main Idea

____

____

Supporting Details

1. ______________________________
2. ______________________________
3. ______________________________

Paragraph 4. Main Idea

____

____

Supporting Details

1. ______________________________
2. ______________________________
3. ______________________________

Mapping

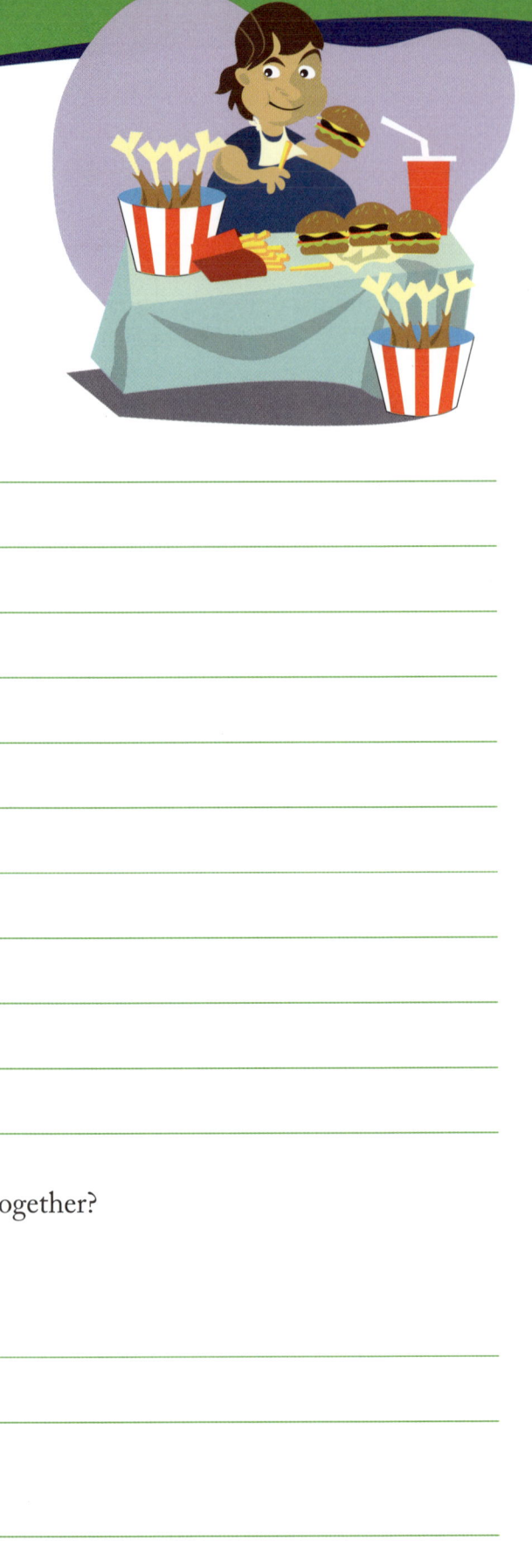

To make your own map, start by writing down everything you know about a topic.

HINT: You don't need to write full sentences.

Topic: Fast Food

WRITE DOWN everything you know about fast food.

Read over your list. Is it mostly details? Can you fit them together?

LIST your main ideas.

Also, WRITE a topic sentence for this topic.

Now, FILL IN this nonfiction story map with the information you wrote down on the previous page.

HINT: Use as many of the boxes as you need. Feel free to add more on a separate piece of paper.

Topic: Fast Food

Topic Sentence

____

Paragraph 1. Main Idea

____

Supporting Details

1. ______________________________
2. ______________________________
3. ______________________________

Paragraph 2. Main Idea

____

Supporting Details

1. ______________________________
2. ______________________________
3. ______________________________

Paragraph 3. Main Idea

____

Supporting Details

1. ______________________________
2. ______________________________
3. ______________________________

Paragraph 4. Main Idea

____

Supporting Details

1. ______________________________
2. ______________________________
3. ______________________________

Cut out the Check It! section on page 215, and see if you got the answers right.

Now it's time to map out the topic you picked on page 209.

Topic: ______________________________

WRITE DOWN everything you know about your topic.

Are you having trouble with your facts? Don't forget to RESEARCH if you need to check the facts or learn some more.

WRITE some questions you still have about your topic.

Where can you GO to answer these questions?

What can you READ to answer these questions?

Who can you ASK to answer these questions?

Now, TURN the page to fill in your map.

Mapping

Now, FILL IN this nonfiction story map with the information you wrote down on the previous page. Don't forget your topic sentence from page 214.

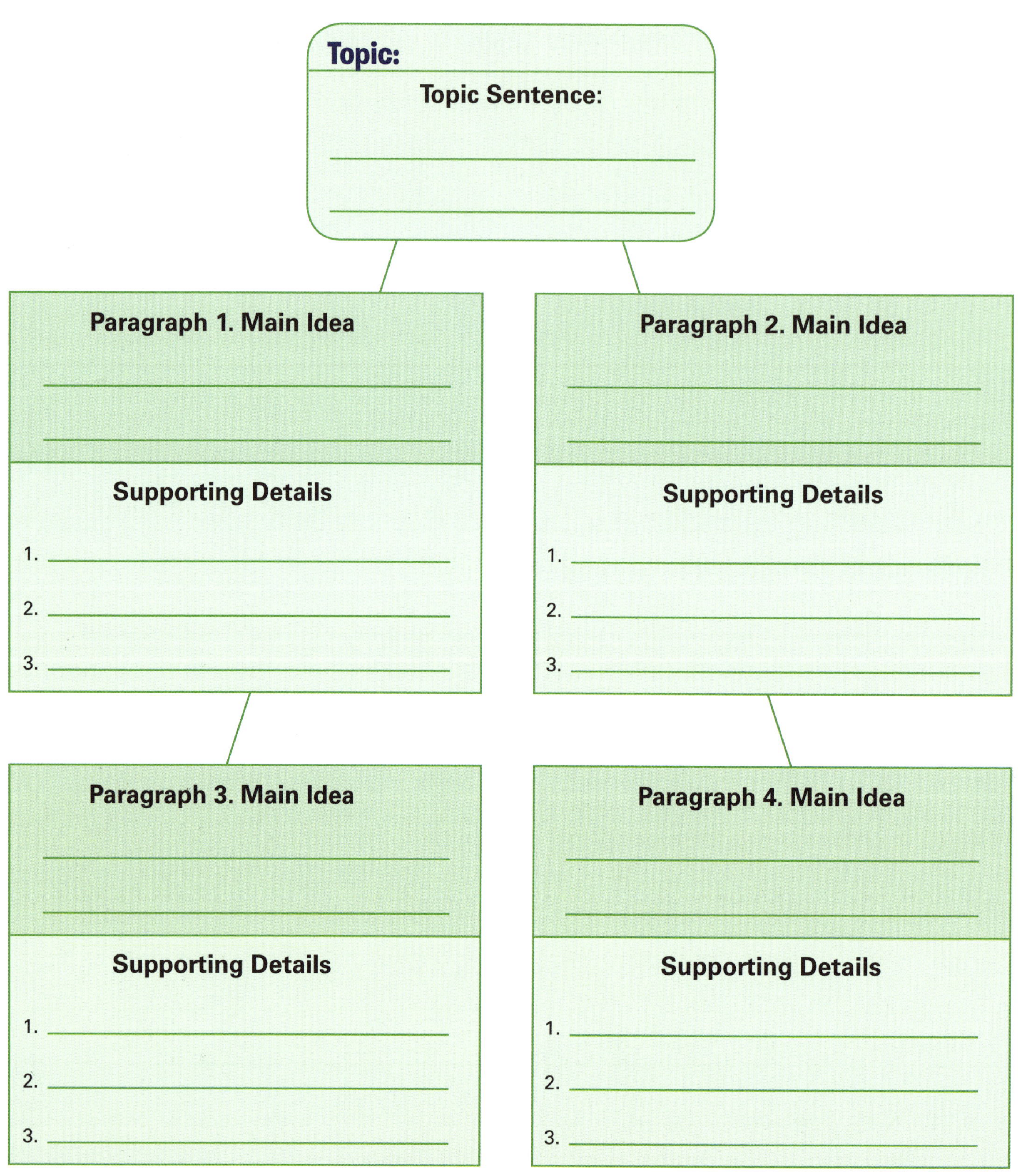

Writing an Argument

Some nonfiction topics give you the chance to express your opinion. When you use facts to support your opinions, you're making an ARGUMENT. A good writer makes strong arguments.

READ this argument story.

It Just Doesn't Make Cents.

Pennies are a waste of money. That's right! It costs almost *two* cents to make one new penny. Pennies aren't even useful. They don't work in gumball machines or arcade games or anything else. Yet every year, we keep making more. You see, the state of Illinois puts up a fight any time somebody tries to make pennies go away. Why? Because President Abraham Lincoln was born in Illinois. (Remember whose face is on the penny?) It simply doesn't make sense to keep making cents. Join the fight!

1. CHECK the author's opinion about pennies.

   ☐ a. The author thinks pennies are useful.

   ☐ b. The author thinks pennies are a waste of money.

LIST the facts that the author uses to support this opinion.

2. ______________________________

3. ______________________________

4. ______________________________

Ta-da! Facts turn an opinion into an argument.

Page 223

1. b
2. It costs more than a penny to make a penny.
3. You can't use pennies in vending machines.
4. Illinois only defends the penny because Abe Lincoln is on it.

Page 224

Suggestions:

Topic: Testing drugs on animals
Testing drugs on animals is wrong because most animal testing labs treat animals badly, and the animals usually die.

Topic: Tearing down the rain forest
Tearing down rain forests is wrong because it can destroy the habitats of entire species, which can lead to extinction.

Topic: People who paint grafitti on walls
People who paint grafitti on walls should be punished severely because they harm other people's property.

Page 225

1. Vote for Benny Howell for karate club president.
2. Give money to the Fund for Polar Bears.

When you're writing an argument, your topic sentence is your opinion. (Look back at the penny story as an example.) It's really important that your readers know right away that you're writing an argument.

FILL IN the blanks to make some quick arguments.

Topic: Kids getting to vote

What's your opinion? Kids should get to vote.

Why? Because the government makes laws that affect kids.

Don't forget to fill in the "Why?" with a fact. That's what makes it an argument.

Topic: Testing drugs on animals

What's your opinion? ______________________

____

Why? ______________________

Topic: Tearing down the rain forest

What's your opinion? ______________________

____

Why? ______________________

Topic: People who paint grafitti on walls

What's your opinion? ______________________

____

Why? ______________________

Those are some good arguments because each one is backed up with facts.

Sometimes you write an argument because you're trying to get your readers to do something. That's when you end your argument with a CALL TO ACTION.

READ these stories. They're missing their calls to action.

Time to Vote

Benny Howell would be a great karate club president. First of all, Benny's been in the club longer than anybody else. Plus, out of all the kids in the club, he ranks the highest in karate skills. Finally, Benny has promised that if he's elected president, he will try to get the karate school to add more classes on Saturdays.

What does the author want you to do?

WRITE the call to action. ______________________________

____

Polar Bears Need YOU!

The Fund for Polar Bears is a really worthy cause. Polar bears don't have as many safe places to float while they search for food because the Arctic ice is shrinking. There are experts who study the ways that global warming affects polar bears. Their research could save the bears, but research costs money and they don't have much of that.

WRITE the call to action. ______________________________

____

Writing an Argument

Here's your chance to map some important arguments.

FILL IN the blanks.

Topic: Your bedtime

Opinion: ______________________________

____

Facts: ______________________________

____

____

____

____

Call to action: ______________________________

____

Topic: Your allowance

Opinion: ______________________________

____

Facts: ______________________________

____

____

____

____

Call to action: ______________________________

____

Topic: Having a pet

Opinion: ______________________________

____

Facts: ______________________________

____

____

____

____

Call to action: ______________________________

____

TURN the page to WRITE your arguments.

HINTS:

1. START with your opinion as the topic sentence.
2. SUPPORT your opinion with facts from the fact list.
3. END by stating your goal and call to action.

Author! Author!

WRITE the argument about your bedtime, using the map on page 226.

Author! Author!

WRITE the argument about your allowance, using the map on page 226.

Author! Author!

WRITE the argument about having a pet, using the map on page 227.

A DRAFT is your first try at writing a story. It's for your eyes only. DRAFTING is when you write a story over and over until you get it right.

First, READ this story map and FILL IN the blanks.

Topic:

Topic Sentence

____

____

Main Idea 1: Indoor Fun

1. Video games
2. Board games
3. ________

Main Idea 2: Outdoor Fun

1. Skateboarding
2. Bike riding
3. ________

Now let's turn this map into a story.

Check It!

Page 231

Suggestions:
Topic: Fun
Topic Sentence: You can have fun inside and out.
Main Idea 1: Indoor Fun
Details:
1. Video games
2. Board games
3. Watching TV

Main Idea 2: Outdoor Fun
Details:
1. Skateboarding
2. Bike riding
3. Playing with a pet

Page 232

Suggestions:
Main Idea 1: There are lots of ways to have fun outside.
Details:
1. You can play video or computer games.
2. You can play board games like checkers.
3. You can watch your favorite TV shows.

Main Idea 2: There are also tons of fun things you can do outside.
Details:
1. Skateboarding, for example, is super fun.
2. There's nothing more fun than riding a bike.
3. If you have a pet, you can play together outside.

Page 233

Suggestion:
You can have fun indoors and out. There are lots of ways to have fun inside the house. You can play video or computer games, for one thing. How about playing a board game like checkers? Of course, you can always watch TV.

Page 234

Suggestion:
If you'd rather have fun in the sun, there's plenty to do outside too. Skateboarding and bike riding, for example, are super fun. If you have a pet, you and Fido can go outside and run around.

No matter where you are, you can find something fun to do if you just look around.

Let's start by turning our main ideas and details into complete sentences.

HINT: A complete sentence has a subject, a verb, and an object.
Example: The *subject* kicked the *object*. (*Kicked* is the verb.)

REWRITE the details from the story map to make them complete sentences.

Main Idea 1: There are lots of ways to have fun outside.

1. You can play video or computer games.
2. __________
3. __________

Main Idea 2: __________

1. __________
2. __________
3. __________

A good story always uses complete sentences.

Now that you've got your sentences, you need to put them together to make paragraphs.

First, REREAD your sentences on the previous page. Then ANSWER these questions.

1. Do all your sentences start with the same words? CIRCLE one: YES NO
   Each sentence should start a different way.

2. Does every detail need its own sentence? CIRCLE one: YES NO
   It's okay to combine some of your details into the same sentence.

WRITE the first paragraph of this story.

HINT: Start with the topic sentence and then Main Idea 1.

Drafting

For the second paragraph, you'll need to start with a TRANSITION. A transition is a way to tell your readers that you're moving to a new main idea. Transitions work between sentences inside a paragraph too. Some transitions are listed in the box.

On the other hand	For example	Of course	However
First of all	Second of all	Next	Then
Finally	Also		

WRITE your second paragraph.

Now we need a CONCLUSION—an ending. It's like the topic sentence, only it's written differently. (If you're writing an argument, the conclusion might be your call to action.)

WRITE your conclusion.

You did it! You wrote a draft.

Let's write another draft. FILL IN this nonfiction story map.

Topic: The People in My Life

Topic Sentence

____

____

Main Idea: My Family

____

____

____

____

____

____

____

____

____

____

____

____

Main Idea: My Friends

____

____

____

____

____

____

____

____

____

____

____

____

TURN the page to write your draft.

HINTS:

1. Write the details into sentences.
2. Combine the sentences into main idea paragraphs.
3. Make the paragraphs flow into each other by using transitions.
4. End with your conclusion.

Author! Author!

WRITE a story draft, using the nonfiction story map on the previous page.

Author! Author!

It's showtime! Using your nonfiction story map from page 222, WRITE a draft of your story.

TURN the page for more space to write.

Drafting

When you make up a story, that's FICTION. You can get your ideas from real life or from your amazing imagination.

Fiction has GENRES like the nonfiction genres we learned about in the first lesson. Do you know any fiction genres?

WRITE DOWN all the kinds of stories you can think of.

Fantasy

What's your favorite genre of story to read?

Check It!

Page 239

Suggestions:
Action/Adventure
Contemporary
Historical
Horror
Humor
Romance
Science fiction
Western

Page 244

1. NOT original
2. Original
3. NOT original
4. Original
5. Original
6. NOT original
7. NOT original
8. Original
9. NOT original
10. Original

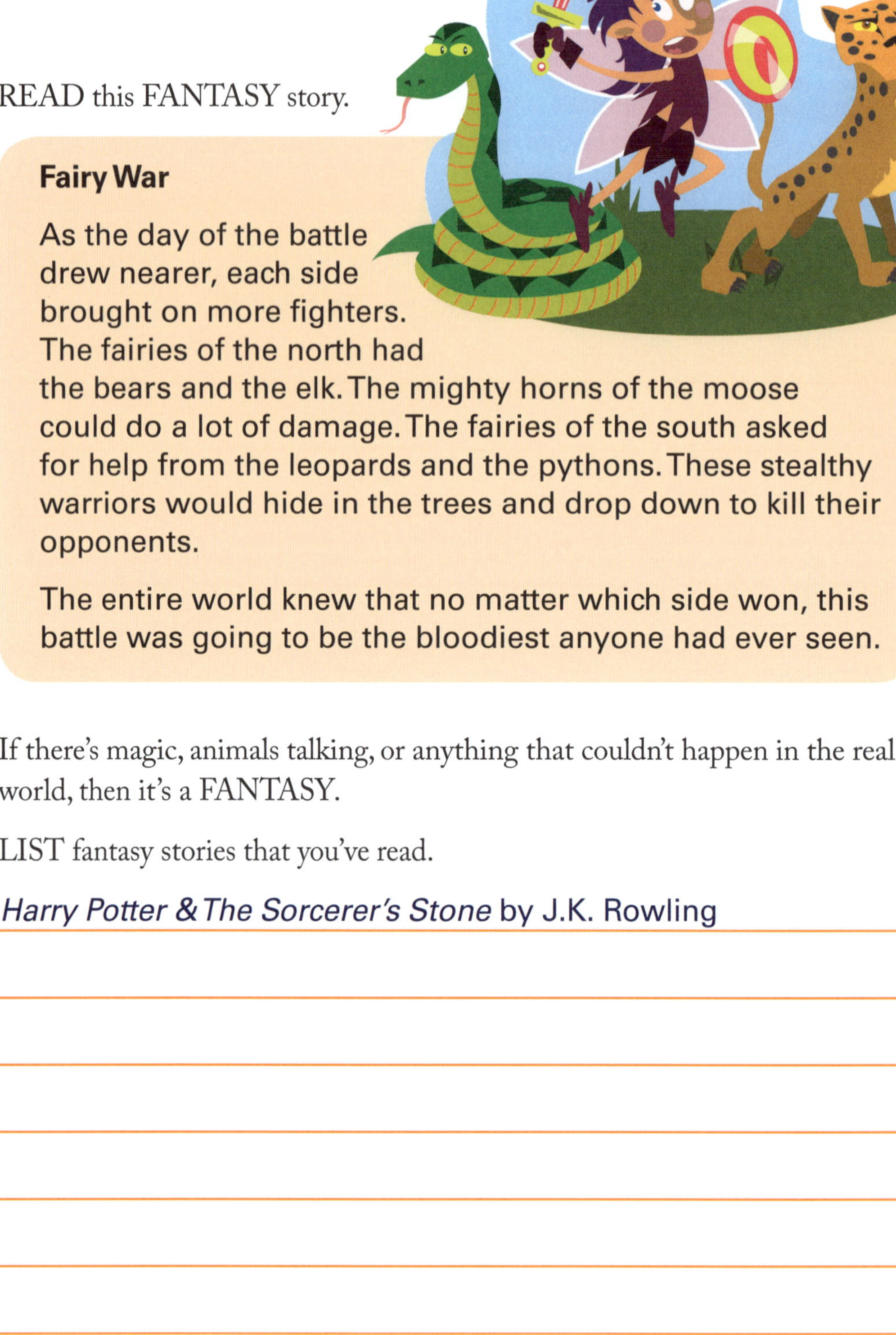

READ this FANTASY story.

Fairy War

As the day of the battle drew nearer, each side brought on more fighters. The fairies of the north had the bears and the elk. The mighty horns of the moose could do a lot of damage. The fairies of the south asked for help from the leopards and the pythons. These stealthy warriors would hide in the trees and drop down to kill their opponents.

The entire world knew that no matter which side won, this battle was going to be the bloodiest anyone had ever seen.

If there's magic, animals talking, or anything that couldn't happen in the real world, then it's a FANTASY.

LIST fantasy stories that you've read.

Harry Potter & The Sorcerer's Stone by J.K. Rowling

READ this HISTORICAL story.

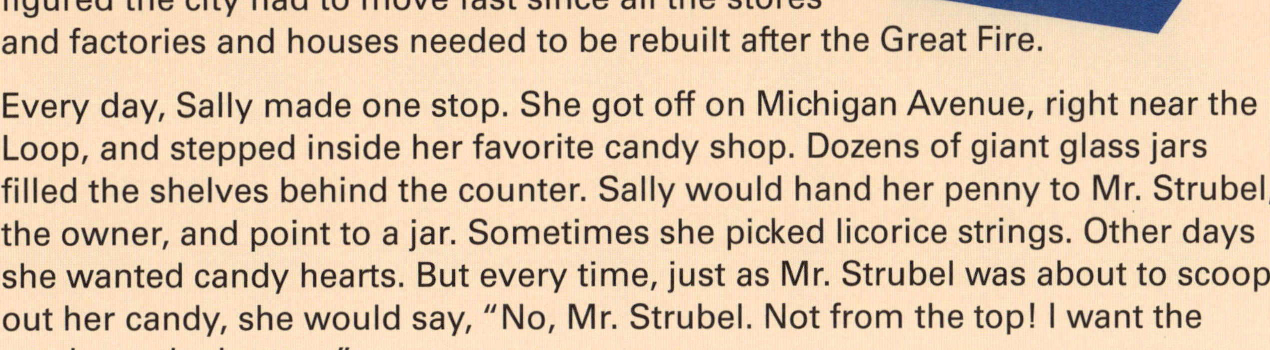

Streetcar Sally

Sally Singleton rode the Chicago streetcars all day. She liked the streetcars better than the new elevated trains because it was easier to watch the people hurrying down the streets from the streetcar. Sally figured the city had to move fast since all the stores and factories and houses needed to be rebuilt after the Great Fire.

Every day, Sally made one stop. She got off on Michigan Avenue, right near the Loop, and stepped inside her favorite candy shop. Dozens of giant glass jars filled the shelves behind the counter. Sally would hand her penny to Mr. Strubel, the owner, and point to a jar. Sometimes she picked licorice strings. Other days she wanted candy hearts. But every time, just as Mr. Strubel was about to scoop out her candy, she would say, "No, Mr. Strubel. Not from the top! I want the candy on the bottom."

Mr. Strubel always groaned when he saw Streetcar Sally come into his shop.

If a story is set in the past, then it's HISTORICAL fiction.

LIST historical stories that you've read.

The Witch of Blackbird Pond by Elizabeth George Speare

READ this HORROR story.

Ghoul School

Alex knew that Ravenwood Elementary was weird the minute he walked through the doors. The halls were so quiet. All the kids just shuffled to their classrooms in silence.

The teachers were even stranger. Alex couldn't tell if they were walking or floating. They moaned in an eerie, echoey way. When they walked by, Alex's hair stood on end and he felt an ice-cold chill. Once he saw a teacher go directly *through* a student!

Alex's mom and dad didn't believe his story, so he waited until the first parent-teacher conference. That night, he tried to warn them one last time. They laughed.

And they never came back.

If a story tries to give you the creeps, then it's a HORROR story.

LIST horror stories that you've read.

The Goosebumps series by R. L. Stine

Many great stories don't seem to have a genre at all. They're called CONTEMPORARY because they're set in the present day—no magic, no aliens, no ghosts.

READ this CONTEMPORARY story.

Earl Does It Again

At Hiawatha Summer Camp, the campers knew one thing for sure. They knew that every Friday Earl would get away and find a way into town. He always found a new way to escape. Once he hid in a hamper filled with dirty sheets going to the laundromat. Another time, he snuck into the backseat of the cook's car as he drove into town for supplies. As soon as Earl got there, he would see a movie, ride his skateboard, and buy a boatload of candy to share with his cabin.

When it got close to dinnertime, Earl would go to see Mrs. Beecher at the post office and use her phone to call the camp. He'd be back in his cabin twenty minutes later.

One day, someone asked him why he bothered coming back at all.

"I have to come back," he said. "Friday is cookout night. I love barbecue!"

LIST contemporary stories that you've read.

Because of Winn-Dixie by Kate DiCamillo

Your story ideas, especially your characters, need to be ORIGINAL. If your idea uses the same names and places that you've seen on TV or read in another book, then they're not original.

CHECK the original ideas in the list.

1. ☐ A sponge named Bob wears square pants and has undersea adventures.
2. ☐ A mouse wants to be an astronaut, so he sneaks onto the space shuttle.
3. ☐ A red monster named Elmo lives on Sesame Street.
4. ☐ Two knights of the Round Table go on a quest to save a princess.
5. ☐ A kid steals a pack of gum from the store and gets caught.
6. ☐ A toy named Buzz Lightyear teams up with his friend Woody for an adventure.
7. ☐ A girl named Dora becomes an explorer with her friend Boots the monkey.
8. ☐ A city of rabbits has to fight off a giant cat.
9. ☐ A kid named Harry Potter finds out he's a wizard.
10. ☐ Five goats form a rock band and travel the world.

Some ideas, like the story of *Little Red Riding Hood*, are so old that it's okay to rewrite them. Stories like that have been around for hundreds of years and have been retold a million times. If you use them, you should always add your own special twist.

You can NEVER copy words directly out of a book for your stories. Never.

Coming up with ideas can be the hardest part about writing.

LIST five ideas for contemporary stories. Remember: no magic, no ghosts, no aliens.

1. ______

2. ______

3. ______

4. ______

5. ______

Now LIST five ideas for fantasy stories.

1. ______

2. ______

3. ______

4. ______

5. ______

Keep coming up with ideas.

LIST five ideas for horror stories. Make them spine-tingling!

1. ______________________________

2. ______________________________

3. ______________________________

4. ______________________________

5. ______________________________

LIST five ideas for historical stories. Think about which time periods you'd like to write about.

1. ______________________________

2. ______________________________

3. ______________________________

4. ______________________________

5. ______________________________

Most good fiction stories have characters that struggle with a problem. Let's take *The Three Little Pigs* as our example.

Who are the characters in *The Three Little Pigs*?
HINT: You can name the characters anything you like.

Where do the three pigs live?
HINT: You can make this up too.

What's the problem in *The Three Little Pigs*?

How do the three pigs solve this problem?

You did it! You just mapped a story.

Check It!

Page 247

Suggestions:
Characters: Larry, Curly, Squiggles, and the Big Bad Wolf
Setting: Piggieville, a suburb of Hogtown
Problem: The wolf keeps blowing the pigs' houses down.
Solution: The pigs hide in a house made of bricks and pour hot oil on the wolf.

Stories are always about CHARACTERS. They don't have to be humans, but they usually act like humans. Good characters want something, like to be treated like a grownup or win the big game.

FILL IN the blanks to make some great characters.

1. Billy ________ is a boy ________
NAME TYPE
who wants to ride a bike ________.
WANTS

2. ________ is a carrot ________
NAME TYPE
who ________.
WANTS

3. Minerva ________ is a ________
NAME TYPE
who wants to rule the world ________.
WANTS

4. ________ is a ________
NAME TYPE
who wants to make a friend ________.
WANTS

5. ________ is a hamster ________
NAME TYPE
who ________.
WANTS

Now you need a place for your characters to hang out. That's called the SETTING. You can make up settings just like you make up characters.

FILL IN the blanks to create fun settings.

1. Tunnelvania (NAME) is a city (TYPE) that's completely underground (DESCRIPTION).

2. ______ (NAME) is a street (TYPE) that's ______ (DESCRIPTION).

3. Hog Hollow (NAME) is a ______ (TYPE) that's where all the pigs live (DESCRIPTION).

4. ______ (NAME) is a ______ (TYPE) that's floating in the sky (DESCRIPTION).

5. ______ (NAME) is a building (TYPE) that's ______ (DESCRIPTION).

Now your characters have an amazing world to explore!

When you write a story, you have to give your characters big PROBLEMS. The best way to make trouble for characters is to make it hard for them to get what they want.

GO BACK to page 248 and make up a story problem for each of the characters. LIST the problems.

Story Problems

Billy can't have a bike because his family is poor.

Phew! That's a lot of problems. Do you feel bad for your characters?

Now comes the good part: You get to solve your characters' problems.

GO BACK to the previous page and make up SOLUTIONS for all of those problems. WRITE the solutions.

Story Solutions

Billy gets a part-time job to save money to buy a bike.

Isn't it fun to make your characters happy in the end?

Fiction Story Map

FINISH the story map, using your fabulous imagination.

Main Character(s)

Renny, a fly who likes to drink soda

Problem

Title

Solution

Setting

Fiction Story Map

FINISH the story map.

Main Character(s)

Problem

Title

Solution

Setting

Blub-Blub,

a city beneath the sea

Fiction Story Map

Use your own great ideas for this story map.

The genre of my story is ______________________________ .

Main Character(s)

____
____
____
____
____

Problem

____
____
____
____
____

Title

____

Solution

____
____
____
____
____

Setting

____
____
____
____
____

PLOT is what happens in a fiction story. You need action and suspense to keep your readers reading.

Let's go back to the *The Three Little Pigs.*

What happens first?

First, the pigs each build a house: one of straw, one of sticks, one of bricks.

What happens next?

____

____

Then what happens?

____

____

Then what happens?

____

____

What do the pigs want?

____

____

How many times do the pigs try to get what they want?

____

Lots of good stories are built like *The Three Little Pigs.*

Page 255

First, the pigs each build a house: one of straw, one of sticks, one of bricks.

Then, the wolf blows down the straw house.

Next, the wolf blows down the stick house.

Then, the wolf tries to blow down the brick house, but he can't.

The pigs want to be safe from the wolf.

They try three times to get what they want.

Page 256

Suggestions:

Stinky puts on perfume.

She rolls around in mud to cover the smell.

She eats a lot of flowers.

Page 257

Suggestions:

Stinky puts on perfume, but the perfume made her smell worse
B

Finally, she tries covering up the smell with mud. The mud works, but she hates being so dirty. She decides she'd rather just be stinky.

Page 258

Suggestions:

Hamlet is loud. Merv is quiet.

First, Hamlet shows how he is louder than Merv.

Merv's so quiet the audience has to sit still to hear him.

Next, Hamlet wears a bright costume so everyone can see him.

Merv uses his sad face to make everyone cry.

Finally, Hamlet gives up and leaves the theater.

Merv tries to do Hamlet's show, but he can't do comedy. Hamlet realizes he's funny and Merv is the serious actor. They become best friends.

Check It!

Page 259

Suggestions:

The girls in Janine's new town have have rolled-up jeans and green shoelaces in their shoes. Janine has wide-legged jeans and white shoelaces.

First, Janine puts green shoelaces in her shoes.

The next day, all the girls have white shoelaces.

Janine buys jeans and wears them rolled up.

The next day, the girls are wearing wide-legged jeans.

Finally, Janine wears all her old clothes. All the girls now fit in with Janine.

It works! She doesn't need to change.

Just like the three pigs, your main character should want something very badly. The plot of your story is what happens when he tries to get what he wants.

Take this character, for example:
Stinky, a skunk who wants to smell pretty

What can Stinky do to get what she wants? LIST things she can try.

She tries to take a bubble bath.

That's a lot of trying! CIRCLE your three favorites.

A story is boring if the main character gets what he wants right away. Some kind of obstacle has to make it hard. That's the story problem. It has to be so hard to solve that the character actually fails the first couple of times he tries.

Let's go back to Stinky the skunk. Do any of her solutions work?

FILL IN the blanks for why Stinky can't lose her smell. (Use what you circled on the previous page.)

What does Stinky try first?

She tries to take a bubble bath. ____________________

Why doesn't it work?

A few minutes after the bath, her smell comes back. __________

What does Stinky try next?

____

Why doesn't it work?

____

Now you've got two choices:

A. Stinky could destink herself.

B. Stinky could fail, but she learns to like herself the way she is, stink and all.

Which do you choose? CIRCLE one: A B

Okay, based on your choice, FILL IN Stinky's final try.

What does Stinky try last?

____

What happens?

____

Plot

Another way to get your story problem started is to bring in a new character, someone who doesn't want your main character to get what he wants.

Here are two new characters for us to work with:

1. Hamlet, a man who wants to be the best actor in his town
2. A guy named Merv who moves to Hamlet's town, claiming to be the best actor

FILL IN the blanks to make Hamlet's story problem.

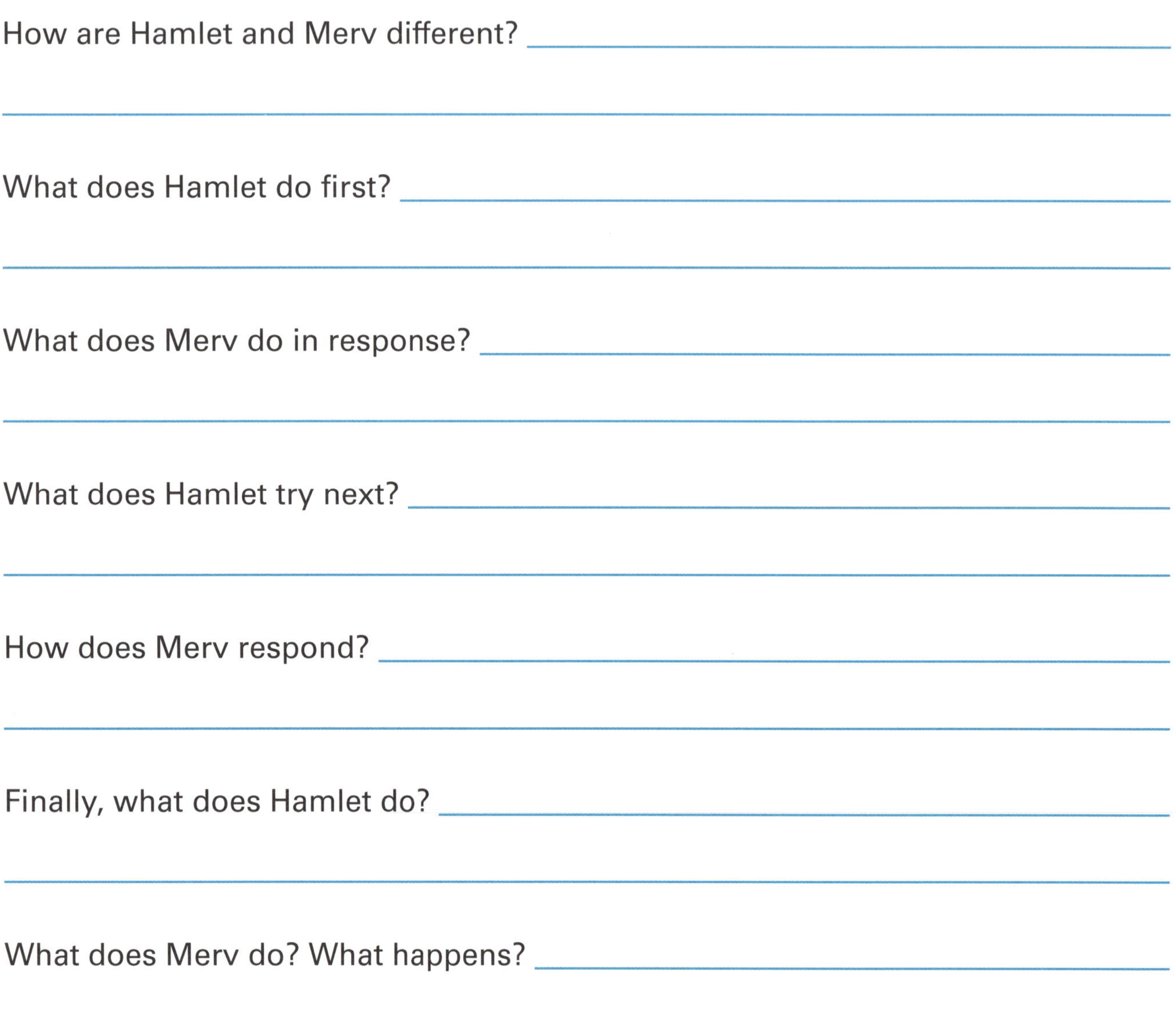

How are Hamlet and Merv different? ______________________________

____

What does Hamlet do first? ______________________________

____

What does Merv do in response? ______________________________

____

What does Hamlet try next? ______________________________

____

How does Merv respond? ______________________________

____

Finally, what does Hamlet do? ______________________________

____

What does Merv do? What happens? ______________________________

____

Each time a character tries to get what he wants and fails, he should try harder the next time, wanting it even more. That way, your readers will get more and more excited.

Another way to cause trouble for your characters is to put them in a new situation, around people and places they don't know (and maybe don't like).

Here's our character:
Janine, a teenager who just moved to a new town and wants to fit in

FILL IN the blanks to make Janine's story problem.

Why does Janine think she doesn't fit in? ______________________________

____

What does she do to fit in first? ______________________________

____

How do people react? ______________________________

____

What does Janine try next? ______________________________

____

What happens? ______________________________

____

Finally, Janine makes one last try. What does she do? ______________________________

____

Does it work? What happens? ______________________________

____

Did you let Janine get what she wanted? You don't *have* to, but if your readers like your character, they probably want her to have a happy ending.

Now, FILL IN this story map, using either Hamlet or Janine's story.

Title ______________________________

The first thing that happens is ______________________________

____

The problem ______________________________

____

After that ______________________________

____

After that ______________________________

____

The solution ______________________________

____

____

Now use the character you chose for your story map on page 254.

______________________ is a ______________________
NAME TYPE

who ____.
WANTS

Now, LIST all the different ways your character could try to get what he or she wants.

CIRCLE your three favorites.
What's the problem? What's keeping your character from winning?

How do you want the story to end?

Now you're ready to fill in your plot map for this story.

Plot

FILL IN this plot map for the story you mapped on page 254.

Title ______________________________

The first thing that happens is ______________________________

____

The problem ______________________________

____

After that ______________________________

____

After that ______________________________

____

The solution ______________________________

____

____

Stories are more than just plot and action. A story also has lots of description and dialogue.

A good DESCRIPTION uses all five senses. READ this description.

Sunday Dinner

Uncle Buck has a voice like a cow mooing. He bellows his questions, like, "So, Danny, how's schoooooool?" Add this to the sound of plates and forks and talk, and you can tell how loud Sunday dinner can be at my house.

On Sundays, the house smells like meat and fried potatoes all day, a smell that sticks to your clothes and hair. Mom turns on the chandelier over the table, and little beams of light shoot all over the room, shining off the dishes and silverware. The Sunday cloth napkins slip off our laps and rub like burlap over our mouths when we wipe our faces.

Dad's roast beef is worth it though. It's not chewy but soft and salty and full of beefy flavor that matches the smell in the air but is ten times better. We wash it down with thick, buttery milk from the farm down the road. I wish Sunday came twice a week!

WRITE the parts of the description that fit each sense.

Smell ____________________

Sound ____________________

Sight ____________________

Taste ____________________

Touch ____________________

Page 263

Smell: meat and fried potatoes
Sound: Uncle Buck's voice, plates and forks and talk
Sight: the light from the chandelier
Taste: Dad's roast beef
Touch: the cloth napkins

Page 264

Suggestions:
Topic: Attics
Smell: dust, moldy clothes, tingling nose wanting to sneeze
Sound: quiet, mice rustling, clunk of a trunk opening
Sight: light coming up through holes in the floor, shadows in the corner, big trunks and boxes
Taste: dry air, cheesy mold, blood from a cut on the finger
Touch: dusty boxes, sharp trunk latch (cuts finger), rough insulation on the ceiling

Page 265

Suggestions:
Topic: Grandma
Smell: heavy perfume, face powder, laundry detergent
Sound: loud nasal voice, jangling jewelry, clicking teeth
Sight: heavy makeup, poofy hair, pointy nails, bright red hair
Taste: perfumey cheek, yummy chicken dinner
Touch: soft skin, bony hand, heavy bracelet

Page 267

1. Terry
2. Pat
3. swimming
4. They're brother and sister.

When you're getting ready to describe an important object or place, take a minute to think about all the ways it can affect your five senses.

FILL IN this sense map about attics.

Topic: Attics

FILL IN this sense map about Grandma.

HINT: This is about a grandmother you make up, not your real granny.

Topic: Grandma

GO BACK to the story you mapped on page 254. PICK a person, object, or place from that story. FILL IN this sense map about your choice.

Topic:

When characters talk to each other in a story, that's called DIALOGUE. You can use dialogue to show what characters are like.

READ this dialogue.

"Yo, what's the hold up?" yelled Pat. "The water's great!"

"I'm coming. The top of my suit's stuck," answered Terry. "Here I am. Oooh, it's cold."

"C'mon, jump in already!"

"Oh no!" cried Terry. "I need to use the stairs."

"Baby!" Pat snorted. "Maybe when you're big like me, you'll be braver."

"I'm not scared."

"Yes, you are."

"I'm telling Mom!"

"Go ahead."

"MOM!"

FILL IN the blanks with information you learned from the dialogue.

1. One of these characters is a girl. Which one is it?

____

2. Which character do you think is older?

____

3. What are these kids doing?

____

4. How are they related?

____

Think about it. How did you know the answers to all those questions?

Author! Author!

WRITE a conversation between a kid and a grownup talking about extreme sports.

HINT: How would they speak differently? Would they use the same kind of words? Would the grownup know as much as the kid?

Author! Author!

WRITE a conversation between two kids sneaking into the kitchen for a midnight snack. Use only dialogue. Let the situation come out through the dialogue.

HINT: What are the kids talking about? Do they have trouble seeing in the dark? What other ways will their situation make them say certain things?

Author! Author!

GO BACK to the story you mapped on page 254. WRITE a dialogue between your main character and somebody else. MIX in some description to show where this conversation is happening. Don't forget to use all five senses.

It's time to write your story draft. You should start by introducing your main character.

Here's one to start with:

Main Character: Percy, a boy who wants to learn to skateboard

FILL IN the blanks.

1. How old is Percy? ______________________

2. What does Percy look like? ______________________

____

____

3. Where does Percy live? ______________________

____

____

4. Why does Percy want to learn to skateboard? ______________________

____

____

5. Where does Percy watch other people skateboarding?

____

____

6. What does he feel when he watches them? ______________________

____

____

____

TURN the page to start writing Percy's story.

Check It!

Page 271

Suggestions:

1. Percy is 12 years old.
2. He has red hair, green eyes, and freckles. His two front teeth are crooked.
3. Percy lives in a suburban neighborhood called Ditmore Heights. The houses are small but separate, with tiny gardens in front.
4. Percy's idol is Vin Kelleher, an older boy who skateboards in the local park every day. All the kids worship him.
5. There's a skateboard park at the end of Percy's street.
6. When Percy watches Vin skateboard, he feels like that's the one thing in the world that makes a boy look cool. If you want anyone to like you, you need to be a skateboard genius.

Page 272

Suggestion:

Percy Stanton is a 12-year-old boy who lives in suburban Ditmore Heights. He has red hair, green eyes, and a bunch of freckles on his nose. There is a skateboard park at the end of his street, and that's where Percy's idol, Vin Kelleher, skates every day. Vin is amazing. He can do anything on a skateboard.

When Percy watches Vin skate, he smiles a little, so that his two crooked front teeth show. Percy wishes he could skate like Vin. Then he would be as cool as Vin, be as grown up as Vin, and have as many friends as Vin. More than anything else in the world, Percy wants to learn to ride a skateboard.

Page 273

Suggestions:

1. Percy's mom is a worrywart.
2. Percy's mom won't let him have a skateboard because she worries that he'll fall off and hurt himself.
3. When Percy's mom thinks about him learning to skateboard, she gets very, very scared. Being scared makes her act angry.

Percy's mom is a worrier. She especially worries about Percy. She worries that he'll be hit by a car if he plays in the street. She worries that he'll be abducted by strangers if he plays in the front yard. She worries he'll be hit by lightning if he plays in the rain. Most of all, she worries that if he gets a skateboard, he'll fall off and get hurt, so she won't let Percy have a skateboard. Whenever he asks her for one, she gets scared and yells at him: "No! Stop asking, Percy. I mean it!"

 Check It!

Page 274

Suggestions:

1. Percy could:
   - borrow a friend's skateboard
   - save up and buy a skateboard
   - convince his mother to let him have one
2. Percy's mom could:
   - take away his friend's skateboard
   - make him return the skateboard he bought
   - forbid Percy to go to the skate park

Page 275

Suggestions:

For the ending, Percy could put his foot down. He could tell his mother that he's twelve years old (or however old you made him), and if he bought a skateboard with his own money, he should be able to keep it and ride it. He could promise that he'll be safe and wear protective gear.

OR: Percy could ask his mother to come with him to the skate park and watch the other kids. Maybe after a little while, she'll feel better about letting Percy ride. They could work out rules for how Percy should be safe.

OR: Percy could give in to his mother and wait to learn to skateboard until he's older.

Page 276

Suggestions:

Percy was angry. His mother didn't have any right to tell him what to buy with his spending money. And he didn't understand why skateboards made her so angry. He took a deep breath and went downstairs to ask her.

She was in the kitchen, banging dishes.

"Mom?" Percy started. "Why are you—"

"I won't listen," Percy's mom said. "I said no and I mean no."

Percy waited for a minute. He took another deep breath. Then he said, "Mom, I'm 12 years old now. I saved up my money to buy that skateboard, and I'm keeping it. I wish you would tell me why it makes you so angry. But I'm going to learn to ride it, no matter what."

Percy's mom started to cry, and Percy felt badly. Finally she told him why she was afraid. She reminded Percy that his father had been a daredevil. He rode a motorcycle and used to jump out of airplanes for fun. Then one day, he had an accident.

"I don't want you to get hurt and leave me all alone!" his mother sobbed.

Percy hugged his mother and promised her that he wouldn't get hurt. He'd be careful and wear pads and a helmet.

"I'll be around for a long time, Ma," he told her. "We're a team."

The next day, he took his new skateboard to the park and asked Vin for a lesson.

WRITE two paragraphs to introduce Percy, his setting, and what he wants most in the world.

Now it's time to introduce Percy's problem.

Problem: Percy's mom won't let him have a skateboard.

FILL IN the blanks.

1. What's Percy's mom like?

____

____

2. Why won't Percy's mom let him have a skateboard?

____

____

3. How does Percy's mom feel when she thinks about Percy learning to skateboard?

____

____

WRITE one paragraph introducing Percy's problem.

____

____

____

____

____

____

____

____

____

Drafting

How can Percy learn to skateboard anyway? Remember, he has to try a couple of times and fail.

1. LIST the ways Percy could try to solve his problem.

2. Now, LIST all the ways Percy's mom could try to stop him.

CIRCLE your favorites and think about how each character feels about what happens.

WRITE two paragraphs about Percy trying to get what he wants and *failing*.

HINT: What does Percy's mom do each time he tries? Or doesn't he tell her?

Drafting

Time to end Percy's struggle. Does Percy finally learn to skateboard? If so, how? What does his mom do about it? Don't forget to show your characters' feelings.

WRITE the ending to Percy's story.

You did it! That's a draft.

Author! Author!

Time to WRITE a draft of your own story.

HINTS:

1. Check your fiction story map on page 254.
2. Use your plot map from page 262.
3. Reread your sense map from page 266.
4. Don't forget the dialogue.

TURN the page for more space to write.

A first draft is never the last. Read it over and look for ways to REVISE it. That means you cut, add, or change things to make your story stronger.

READ this story.

All That Jazz

Jazz is all-American music. It was invented in the United States. While other musicians play from sheet music that tells them which notes to play, jazz musicians *improvise*. That means they make up notes as they go along, so they play the songs differently each time. Jazz players never play a song the same way twice.

Another thing that makes jazz special is its rhythm. Jazz music uses *syncopation*, which is when a song hits an unexpected beat. Instead of BAH-buh-BAH-buh-BAH-buh, a jazz song might go buh-BAH-BAH-buh-buh-BAH. That's not the type of rhythm you'll hear in classical music. It's not used in many older kinds of music. Even though jazz music has been around long enough to be considered classical, it still sounds fresh and new.

This story is too long. CROSS OUT **three** sentences that aren't necessary.

HINT: Why say the same thing twice?

Check It!

Page 279

Cut these sentences:

1. It was invented in the United States.
2. Jazz players never play a song the same way twice.
3. It's not used in many older kinds of music.

Page 280

Suggestion:
Some people love chocolate so much they'll take a bath in it. At the Hotel Hershey in Hershey, Pennsylvania, chocolate lovers pay $40 to splash around in whipped cocoa for 15 minutes. For only $65, these fanatics can get a chocolate sugar scrub. For an hour-long cocoa rubdown to relax their muscles, customers need to cough up $120. Now *that's* a chocolate lover!

Page 281

Suggestion:
Flamingoes are like birds from fantasyland with their pink-orange color, long legs and neck, and a bill that turns down at the tip. They almost always stand on one leg with the other tucked underneath. You might think they're going to fall over, but they don't. Who knows why they stand that way? Maybe that's how they keep warm. They might stand like that to keep at least one foot dry all the time since they stand in water a lot. Flamingoes are an unsolved mystery.

Page 282

Suggestion:
Princess Ballia hated being a princess. She hated the fancy clothes, the boring parties, and living in the coldest castle in the world. Most of all, Princess Ballia hated the rules. There were 1,100 rules for being a princess, and she had to memorize every single one of them.

One day, Princess Ballia decided to escape. She cut her long blonde hair into a short style like a boy's. She put on a cap to shade her blue eyes and wore a pair of rough pants and a shirt instead of her usual gown.

"I don't look anything like myself," she said. "Now I can just walk right out of here."

Page 283

Suggestion:

The sharp smell of nail polish told Eli that his sister Marcella was in her room, painting her nails. He threw open her door and grabbed her by the arm.

"You've got to come downstairs!" he cried.

She pulled back. "What are you doing? You'll wreck my primary coat!"

Eli ignored her and dragged her down the stairs. His heart was pounding and he was breathing hard, so it was difficult to talk, but he tried anyway.

"There's a big thing in the backyard," he gasped. "It just landed."

"What kind of big thing?" Marcella asked. They were stumbling by the family photos in the front hallway, and she knocked one off the wall as they passed.

"It's a big spaceship kind of thing," Eli answered as they went through the kitchen.

"A what?" Marcella tried to wrench her arm out of her brother's grip. "Stop fooling around! Why do you have to be such a—"

By this time, they were in the backyard, and she could see for herself.

Page 284

Suggestion:

What else could Olivia try instead of flour?

She could use baking powder. What would that taste like?

She could use face powder. What would that smell like?

OR:

Where could Olivia look for flour?

She could go to the store. How would she get there?

She could ask a neighbor. Are her neighbors weird?

When you're revising your nonfiction story, make sure that your main idea is crystal clear.

READ this story.

Extreme Chocolate Lovers

Some people like baths filled with smelly oils or goopy mud. Why not add chocolate? At the Hotel Hershey in Hershey, Pennsylvania, you can pay $40 to splash around in whipped cocoa for 15 minutes. But can you really get clean in a chocolate bath? Please, don't drink the bath water when you get out. You can also spend $120 on an hour-long cocoa rubdown to relax your muscles. Maybe you'd prefer a chocolate sugar scrub for $65? Don't worry, you can have all this "choco-therapy" without gaining a pound!

The main idea of this story is extreme chocolate lovers. REVISE the story so that the main idea is clear.

HINTS: Rewrite the topic sentence. Cut and rearrange the rest.

Is your story fun to read? Make sure every sentence starts in a different way, and don't repeat the same words all the time.

READ this story.

Pink Flamingoes

Flamingoes are like birds from fantasyland. They're a pink-orange color and have long legs, a long neck, and a bill that turns down at the tip. They almost always stand on one leg with the other leg tucked underneath. They look like they're going to fall over, but they don't. Who knows why they stand that way? Maybe that's how they keep warm. Maybe that's how they keep at least one foot dry all the time since they stand in water a lot. Flamingoes are an unsolved mystery.

REVISE this story so that you're not repeating words and sentence starters.

HINTS: Use some transitions from page 234. It's okay to combine two sentences into one.

Rereading & Revising

Have a friend read your fiction story. Does the main character feel like a real person to your reader? If not, you may need to add more detail.

READ this paragraph.

Plucky Princess

Princess Ballia hated being a princess. She thought it was terrible. So one day, she hid in the back of a cart and escaped into the outside world. Luckily she wasn't caught.

REVISE this paragraph so that the main character is more real.

HINT: Add detail to introduce your reader to Princess Ballia. What does she look like? Why does she hate being a princess? How did she get the idea (and courage) to escape?

Description and dialogue make you *show* a scene rather than just *tell* about it.

READ this paragraph.

Aliens at Eli's House

Eli ran into the house. He found his sister Marcella in her room, painting her nails. He told her he needed her help—fast! As they ran down the stairs, he explained what had happened in the backyard. She didn't believe him until she saw it for herself—an alien spaceship had landed right in Mom's flower beds!

REVISE this scene to make it *show* rather than *tell*.

HINT: Add dialogue, and use your five senses to describe where the characters are and how they feel.

When you reread your fiction story, pay attention to the ending. Does it come too fast?

READ this story.

Olivia's Big Mistake

"I'm going to bake a cake," Olivia announced one day when her parents were away.

First, Olivia put all of the ingredients on the kitchen table. She couldn't find any flour, so she used salt instead.

"Nobody will notice the difference," she said.

After dinner that night, Olivia served her cake. Her family spit it out.

"I guess you noticed the difference," Olivia said sadly.

REVISE the ending of this story so that it doesn't come so quickly.

HINT: Did Olivia try hard enough to solve her problem?

Author! Author!

REREAD and REVISE your nonfiction story draft from page 237. WRITE the revised version here.

TURN the page to finish revising your story.

The final step to a finished story is PROOFREADING. That's when you carefully check for mistakes in spelling, punctuation, and grammar. Then you EDIT the mistakes by fixing them.

READ this story.

I Scream for Ice Cream

I love ice cream. I also happin to be a total expert on the suject. Trust me—during my thirten years on this planet, I've tried it all: forzen custard, frozen yogurt, sorbet, and gelato. But plain old icecream will always reign supreem with me. When it comes to flavors, I like to mix it up a little. Give me plain old vanilla, but top it off with choclate sauce, or buttsercortch, or razzberry syrup. And don't forget teh whipped cream!

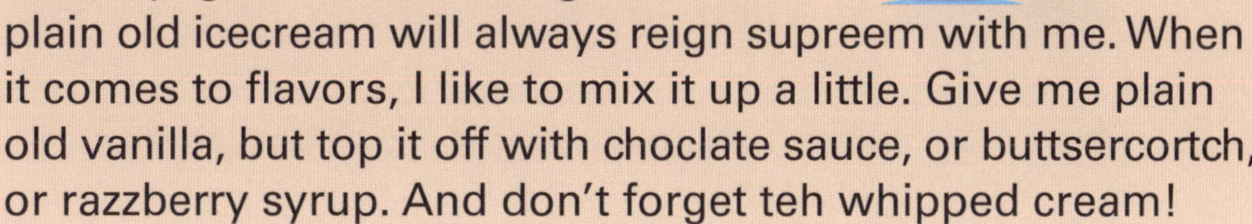

CIRCLE the 10 spelling errors in the story.

HINT: Use a dictionary to check words you don't know. WRITE the correct words in the blanks.

1. ______________________
2. ______________________
3. ______________________
4. ______________________
5. ______________________
6. ______________________
7. ______________________
8. ______________________
9. ______________________
10. ______________________

Check It!

Page 287

1. happen
2. subject
3. thirteen
4. frozen
5. ice cream
6. supreme
7. chocolate
8. butterscotch
9. raspberry
10. the

Page 289

Connor's Sick Day

One morning, Connor decided to be sick, so he stayed in bed.

"Connor, time for school," his dad said.

Connor just groaned.

A few **minutes** later, Connor's mom came to get him.

"Connor, time for school," she said.

"I don't feel well," Connor said. He tried to look very sick.

It worked! Connor stayed home while his parents **wont** to work.

First, he watched TV, but there wasn't anything good on. Next, he made himself a sandwich out of peanut butter, chocolate sauce, and **marshmallows**. Then, he played **video** games for three hours. Finally, he made a milkshake with strawberries, frozen yogurt, lemon-lime soda, and butterscotch.

When his parents **came** home from work, Connor was back in bed.

"Do you feel better, honey?" his mom asked.

Connor groaned and grabbed his stomach. "No, I feel much worse."

When you proofread your story, you can use special proofreading marks to flag the mistakes. Then you can find them and fix them.

^ When something's missing you can add it using this mark.

⊙ Use this mark to add a period.

≡ did you forget to capitalize a letter? use this mark.

/ To Make a letter lowercase instead, uSe this Mark.

ℓ To to cut something, use that this mark.

¶ Want to make a new paragraph? ¶ Use this mark.

Page 290

"Howdy, Ajax!" cried Bambo.
"Yo, Bambo," said Ajax. He sighed.
"What's wrong?" Bambo asked.
Ajax said, "Everything's wrong today."
"Well," said Bambo. "What's the worst thing?"
Ajax thought for a minute. "It's the first thing in the morning," he said.

PROOFREAD this story, using proofreading marks.

HINT: Watch the verb tenses.

Connor's Sick Day

One morning, Connor decided to be sick, so he stayed in bed.

"connor, time for school," his dad Said.

Connor just groaned

A few minurtes later, Connors mom came to get him.

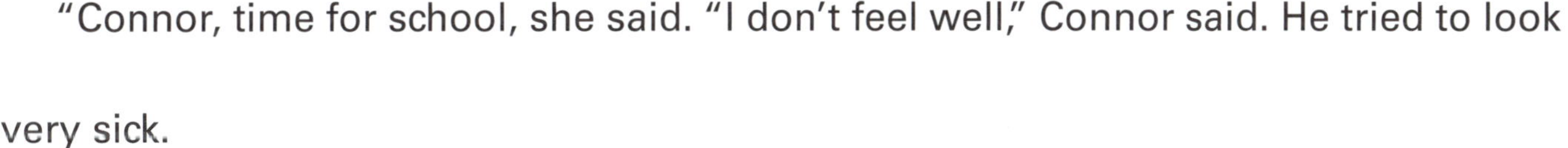

"Connor, time for school, she said. "I don't feel well," Connor said. He tried to look very sick.

It worked! Connor stayed hoMe while his parents to work. first, he watchd TV, but there wasn't anything good on. Next, he made himself a sandwich out of peanut butter chocolate sauce, and marshmalows. Then, he play video video games for three hours Finally, he made a Milkshake with strawberries, frozen yogurt lemon-lime soda, and butterscotch.

When his parents are came home from work, Connor was back in Bed.

"Do you feel better, honey" his mom asked.

Connor groan and grabbed his stomach. "No, I feel much worse."

Proofreading & Editing

Dialogue can be tricky. You need to make sure the quotation marks and punctuation are in the right place. Look inside any fiction book to see how it works.

Here's the RIGHT way to do it.

"How's my hair?" asked John.

"I think it looks great," said Annie.

"I don't know." John shook his head. "Maybe it's too fluffy."

Annie replied, "Fluffy is cute."

"Yuck!" John ran out of the room to wet his head again.

PROOFREAD this dialogue, using proofreading marks.

"Howdy, Ajax" cried Bambo!

"Yo, Bambo. said Ajax. He sighed."

"What's wrong," Bambo asked? Ajax said "everything's wrong today."

"Well" said Bambo "What's the worst thing?" Ajax thought for a minute.

It'sthe first thing in the morning, he said.

Now, EDIT it. That means REWRITE the dialogue so that all the errors are fixed.

Author! Author!

It's time to polish your own work. First, proofread and edit your nonfiction story from pages 285 and 286. Then, WRITE the final draft here.

TURN the page to finish your final draft.

Author! Author!

Now, revise, proofread, and edit your fiction story from pages 277 and 278. WRITE the final draft here.

TURN the page to finish your final draft.

When you share your story with the world, you PUBLISH it. You already know lots of ways to publish a story.

1. LIST three ways stories are published in PRINT.

comic books

2. LIST three ways stories are published on FILM or TV.

cartoons

3. LIST three ways stories are published on the INTERNET.

online journals (blogs)

4. LIST three ways stories are PERFORMED live.

puppet shows

Check It!

Page 295

Suggestions:

1. **Print:**
   - magazines
   - books
   - newspapers
2. **Film or TV:**
   - sitcoms
   - movies
   - newscasts
   - documentaries
3. **Internet:**
   - online videos
   - Web sites
   - online news magazines
4. **Live performance:**
   - plays
   - read alouds
   - radio news shows

Author! Author!

WRITE a paragraph about your town for a national magazine read by grownups.

An e-mail you send to your best buddy is going to sound a lot different than a letter you write to your grandma, right? You should always remember your readers when you're writing or publishing a story.

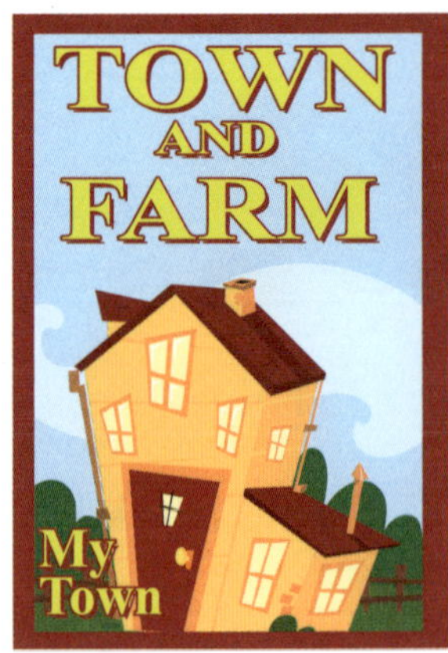

This time, WRITE a paragraph about your town for a local kids Web site. What will be different?

LIST places where you could publish your nonfiction story from pages 291 and 292.

LIST places where you could publish your fiction story from pages 293 and 294.

Now you know where to start. Good luck!

Now you know it all, right? Prove it!

Let's start with an argument.

Topic: Kids having jobs

Opinion: ______________________________

____

Facts: ______________________________

____

____

____

Do you need a call to action?

If so, WRITE it here. ______________________________

____

____

Now, TURN the page to WRITE your argument.

HINTS:

1. START with your opinion as the topic sentence.
2. SUPPORT your opinion with facts from the fact list.
3. END by stating your goal and call to action.

Author! Author!

WRITE your argument about kids having jobs, using the map on the previous page.

Now, REREAD and REVISE your argument.

HINTS:

1. Is your opinion stated clearly?
2. Do all your sentences start differently?
3. How many facts do you use to support your argument?
4. Don't forget to cut sentences you don't need.

Nonfiction Review

Time to write a nonfiction story.

First, PICK a genre. ______________________________

HINT: See some choices on pages 200 through 203.

Next, PICK a topic.

Big Topic: ______________________________

Smaller Topics:

____

____

____

CIRCLE the topic you want to write about.

WRITE your topic sentence. ______________________________

____

____

LIST all the facts you know about this topic.

HINT: Don't forget to research if you need to.

____

____

____

____

____

____

FILL IN this story map, using the facts from the previous page.

Topic:

Topic Sentence:

____

____

Paragraph 1. Main Idea

____

____

Supporting Details

1. ______________________________
2. ______________________________
3. ______________________________

Paragraph 2. Main Idea

____

____

Supporting Details

1. ______________________________
2. ______________________________
3. ______________________________

Paragraph 3. Main Idea

____

____

Supporting Details

1. ______________________________
2. ______________________________
3. ______________________________

Paragraph 4. Main Idea

____

____

Supporting Details

1. ______________________________
2. ______________________________
3. ______________________________

Author! Author!

Now you've got what it takes! WRITE your first draft of this new nonfiction story. Use the map on page 303.

HINTS:

1. Write the details into sentences.
2. Combine the sentences into main idea paragraphs.
3. Make the paragraphs flow into each other.
4. End with your conclusion (or your call to action).

TURN the page to start your final draft.

Nonfiction Review

Now, REREAD your story draft.

FILL IN the blanks to come up with a plan for revision.

1. Is your topic sentence boring or unclear? WRITE another version here.

____

____

2. Do each of your paragraphs have a main idea? LIST them.

   Paragraph 1 Main Idea: ______________________

   Paragraph 2 Main Idea: ______________________

   Paragraph 3 Main Idea: ______________________

   Paragraph 4 Main Idea: ______________________

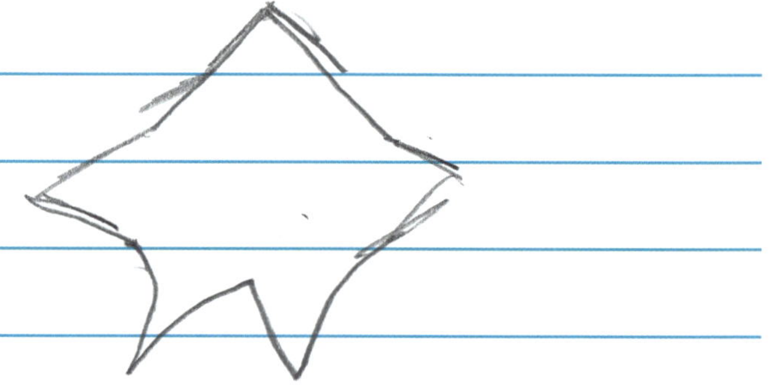

3. Do all your sentences start differently? Are you using transitions? UNDERLINE any sentences that need to be rewritten.

4. Does your story end with a strong conclusion or call to action? WRITE a strong ending sentence here.

____

____

5. Are all of your facts correct? RESEARCH one new fact and WRITE it here.

____

____

Now you're ready to revise.

Author! Author!

REVISE your nonfiction story, using your notes from the previous page.

TURN the page to finish your final draft.